AF706186

Challenges for Human Rights

Nijhoff Law Specials

VOLUME 71

Challenges for Human Rights

by

Fernando Falcón y Tella

Translated into English by
Howard Shneider from
Nuevos retos de los derechos humanos
Madrid, Grupo Difusion, 2006
Final revision by the author.

MARTINUS
NIJHOFF
PUBLISHERS

LEIDEN • BOSTON
2007

Printed on acid-free paper.
A C.I.P. record for this book is available from the Library of Congress.

ISBN: 978 9004 16022 4

© 2007 by Koninklijke Brill NV, Leiden, The Netherlands.
Koninklijke Brill NV incorporates the imprints Brill, Hotei Publishers, IDC Publishers, Martinus Nijhoff Publishers and VSP.

http://www.brill.nl

All rights reserved. No part of this publication may be reproduced, stored in a retrieval system, or transmitted in any form or by any means, electronic, mechanical, photocopying, microfilming, recording or otherwise, without written permission from the Publisher.

Authorization to photocopy items for internal or personal use is granted by Brill provided that the appropriate fees are paid directly to The Copyright Clearance Center, 222 Rosewood Drive, Suite 910, Danvers MA 01923, USA.
Fees are subject to change.

Printed and bound in The Netherlands.

For Professor José Iturmendi Morales

Table of Contents

Foreword

A recurring theme among the reflections of Norberto Bobbio is the consideration that human rights "*are historical rights, which is to say that they emerged in certain circumstances, marked by struggles in favor of the defense of new freedoms against old powers, and in a gradual fashion that did not occur all at once*" (N. Bobbio, *L'età dei diritti*, Torino, 1990). For instance, religious freedom is the result of the religious wars, civil liberties came from the struggles of parliaments against absolute sovereignty, political and social freedoms were born, developed, and grew from wage-earning workers movements, and so on. Certain demands are born, in fact, only when certain necessities are born, and new necessities are born in correlation with changes in social conditions.

As a result, to confront the subject of new challenges in human rights, in the first place it is necessary—as Professor Fernando Falcón y Tella correctly does—to look at the society that surrounds us, a society that in recent decades has experienced profound and extremely rapid transformations. Large migratory flows from the poorest countries in the world to industrialized nations have changed the features of old nation states, creating a situation marked by legal pluralism and opening new dimensions to legal operators—legislatures and judges. The birth and consolidation of supranational structures have brought about a redefining of familiar concepts such as those of sovereignty and citizenship. The education level of women has grown notably, and has resulted in a considerable improvement in their living conditions. Nonetheless, although the law formally recognizes complete equality between both sexes, there still exist large differences regarding issues such as the type of job or level of studies that men and women have. Research in the area of biomedicine, and in the scientific realm in general, every day offers greater possibilities of dominating nature (e.g. artificial insemination, organ transplants, cloning, etc.). In turn, this potential leads to the emergence of painful questions regarding the limits of interventionism in human and nonhuman life—animals and the environment—and regarding whether it is suitable or not for the law to regulate such issues. Computer technology has entered into our lives at all levels, resulting in a kind of revolution, compared by some to the revolution sparked by the invention of the printing press, and giving rise to urgent necessities regarding the protection of privacy. All of these phenomena, dealt with in the book, have opened new frontiers and have given rise to new challenges in relation to certain ideologies, especially regarding the scientific doctrine.

One of the fields in which these transformations have influenced things in a more profound way is, as is emphasized throughout this study, that of human rights. In recent decades we have witnessed a process of specification regarding the subjects of human rights and have seen the multiplication of human rights typologies.

The individual subjects of today are not just the old traditional ones, in which people were considered in an abstract light, but rather subjects placed in a context. In other words, individuals today are seen in their precise, specific nature with respect to the diverse ways of existing in society. Examples of this new conception include viewing the individual in conditions of difficulty (e.g. sick, downtrodden, etc.) or as a victim of social discrimination due to historical causes (e.g. women, blacks, etc.). On the other hand, the ownership of rights is often attributed not only to individual subjects, but rather to groups, peoples and nations—to an increasingly larger base of subjects, including *future generations*, and also nonhuman subjects such as animals and the environment.

Amongst new subjects the biggest problems of classification emerge in relation to future generations and embryos, as well as with respect to non-human subjects, animals and the environment.

Regarding future generations, there have arisen doubts about the possibility of giving rights to beings that still do not exist and are not even in the making. Considering that nobody even knows if such beings will exist one day, and if they do exist, what they will be like, it is hard to know if these beings deserve rights. In the case of an embryo, the key point is the moment from which it can be considered a human being for all intents and purposes. Regarding animals, of particular interest are the reflections of Tom Regan, who tries to construct a new theory of laws, animals and non-animals, starting from the distinction between moral agents—rational, adult human beings—and passive moral subjects—all human beings with consciousness and feeling, which is to say those who are capable of experiencing pleasure or pain and have hopes, memories and emotions. Regarding the environment, those who begin from an anthropocentric perspective consider nature as property in the service of man, and think that it must be protected for reasons of utility. For others, who approach the matter using a biological analysis, nature is an entity endowed with intrinsic value.

The other direction in which the theory and practice of human rights has developed in recent years is that of its multiplication. This has occurred to the point that in some cases it seems inappropriate to even speak of rights. Nonetheless, in such cases the designation is still maintained, as Norberto Bobbio points out, in order to grant a title of integrity and greater force to certain ideal aspirations in light of the regulation they will help provide.

A broad catalogue of human rights has been sketched, with unclear boundaries, that includes the hope for a heterogeneous framework that covers: the right to peace, the right of development, the right of cultural identity, the right of privacy against potential interference with information, the right to die with dignity instead of through therapeutic cruelty, or the right to the integrity of one's own genetic patrimony, amongst other.

The merit of this book by Fernando Falcón y Tella is that in it he has examined all of these complex phenomena from an interdisciplinary viewpoint, starting from the level of the facts, which is to say from the level of social transformations—multiculturalism, globalization and the impact of new technologies, as much so computer-based as biomedical. After this examination of the factual level, the author goes on to explore the normative and axiological dimensions of the aforementioned phenomena, and in this way follows the three-dimensional method.

Carla Faralli
Professor of Legal Philosophy
University of Bologna

I Introduction

In recent years we have witnessed a kind of revolution, a turning point in history, in the field of human rights. Despite the existence of permanent abuses as well as flagrant violations of human rights, international law has not been applied to such issues because the states where said violations occurred have declared themselves sovereign. This sovereignty allows the states to remain immune to external or internal responsibility or interference. One of the classic characteristics of sovereignty is freedom from the potential interference of foreign powers and another such characteristic is the state's ability to be the final decision-maker, thus preventing any type of legal recourse in the internal realm to challenge the state's resolutions. However, despite the presence throughout history of such situations, today we are fortunate enough to be experiencing a boom in human rights—an enormous increase of their importance in the international sphere at all levels (political, economic, social, legal and moral). For the first time the condition of the individual as "citizen," and not just as "subject," has gained importance. Individuals, and not only states, have now become the subjects of international law, as a result of the boom in humanitarian law and international criminal law. This study will examine, among other issues, the International Criminal Court, which protects *individual* victims by punishing *individual* human rights offenders.

However, although there have been many battles won and goals met concerning human rights, the war against injustice continues and the fight has not ended. It is necessary to stay alert and to avoid a potentially paralyzing self-complacency. We have come a long way, but there is still a long way to go. There are still many barriers to overcome on the path to securing human rights. To complete this path it is necessary to have a vision of the future and to put forth a constant effort, while at the same refusing to get discouraged.

What are these barriers that must be overcome?[1] Putting aside the peculiarities and specific problems of each nation as well as a series of frequent problems in the fight for human rights (e.g. gender discrimination [to which we will only refer to in passing], race or religion, difficulties in access to education, torture,[2] etc.), in this book I would like to focus on other topics that are particularly relevant with respect to the most recent period in our history. This being the case, I will examine issues such as multiculturalism, globalization, international criminal justice[3] (specifically third and fourth generation rights) and, within this thematic framework, the problems that have come about as a result of the expanding reach of the Internet and of new biomedical advances. In addition, this study will explore the increasingly urgent challenge of how to respond to international terrorism, in view of the most recent worldwide events since September 11 and its resulting aftermath.

1 Paul Gordon Lauren, "Nuevos retos para los derechos humanos. El futuro a la luz del pasado," conference given at the II Jornadas Internacionales "Nuevos retos de los derechos humanos," held by the Instituto de Derechos Humanos, in November, 2003, at the Facultad de Derecho de la Universidad Complutense de Madrid. Spanish translation from the original English version: "New Challenges for Human Rights: The Future in Light of the Past," translated by Fernando Falcón y Tella, published in the *Anuario de Derechos Humanos del Instituto de Derechos Humanos de la Facultad de Derecho de la Universidad Complutense de Madrid. Nueva Época*, vol. 5, 2004, pp. 369-386, esp. pp. 369-371.

2 Regarding the topic of torture, see, among other authors, Beatriz Castro Toledo, "Consideraciones sobre la licitud e ilicitud de la tortura," in Various Authors, *El concepto de relevancia jurídica (Estudios de la Sección de Filosofía del Derecho. Real Academia de Jurisprudencia y Legislación)*, Madrid, Centro de Estudios Registrales, 2001, pp. 249-263. Torture was also the theme examined in this professor's doctoral thesis.

3 Highlighting the existing link between globalization and international justice, see Angela Del Vecchio, *Giurisdizione internazionale e globalizzazione. I tribunali internazionali tra globalizzazione e frammentazione*, Milano, Giuffrè, 2003. And Pedro R. David, *Globalización, prevención del delito y justicia penal*, Buenos Aires, Zavalia, 1999.

II A Study of Some of the Main Challenges Currently Presented to Human Rights

1 Multiculturalism and Human Rights

1.1 What Is Meant by Multiculturalism as a Contemporary Phenomenon?

The theory and practice of what currently is referred to as multiculturalism[1] developed, beginning in the 1980s, originally in the United States of America[2] and afterwards in Europe. This development oc-

1 Concerning multiculturalism, see Gerd Bauman, *El enigma multicultural*, Barcelona, Paidós, 2001. Anna Elisabetta Galeotti, *Multiculturalismo. Filosofia politica e conflitto identitario*, Napoli, Liguori, 1999. Christian Joppke – Steven Lukes (eds.), *Multicultural Questions*, Oxford, Oxford University Press, 1999. B. Parekh, *Rethinking Multiculturalism. Cultural Diversity and Political Theory*, London, 2000; which has the Spanish translation, *Repensando el multiculturalismo. Diversidad cultural y teoría política*, Madrid, Istmo. Giovanni Sartori, *La sociedad multiétnica. Pluralismo, multiculturalismo y extranjeros*, Madrid, Taurus, 2001. Ayelet Achachar, "Multicultural Vulnerability," in Christian Joppke – Steven Lukes (eds.), *Multicultural Questions, op. cit.*, pp. 87-111.

2 Among other anglosaxon authors that deal with this topic, directly or tangentially, other than those authors already cited, of particular importance is Ronald M. Dworkin, professor at *New York University* and *London University*, in his emblematic work *Taking Rights Seriously*, London, Duckworth & Co. Ltd., 3ª ed, 1981; there is a Spanish translation by Marta Guastavino, *Los derechos en serio*, Barcelona, Ariel, 1984. Barcelona, Planeta-Agostini, 1992. *Id. Ética privada e igualitarismo político*, Spanish translation by Antoni Domènech, Barcelona, Paidós, 1993. *Id.* "Do Liberal Values Conflict?", in Ronald M. Dworkin (*et al.*) (eds.), *The Legacy of Isaiah Berlin*, New York, New York Review of Books, 2001,

curred during the recent boom in migratory phenomena and the simultaneous revival of nationalism. Leaving aside its possible variants, one can affirm that multiculturalism is clearly a theoretical creation of the United States, unlike the phenomenon of pluralism, which emerged from a distinctly European school of thought.[3] At the same time, it's necessary to distinguish between the multiculturalism that is defended in the U.S. and that which is defended in Canada. In Canada, the central axle around which the controversy of multiculturalism turns is the problem of Quebec. In this Canadian region, the debate deals with the recognition of the peculiarities of Quebec's population due to its culturally French origins. On the other hand, in the United States the theme of multiculturalism is related to the coexistence of distinct races—the African American minority, which came about as a consequence of the massive incorporation of slaves from west Africa and which later led to the current problems relating to the black minority in the U.S.; the Spanish, that came to the country as a consequence of large waves of immigration; the Native American population, that gave rise to the "Indian question"; and an Anglo-Saxon elite that maintains its influence in circles of power and decision-making.[4]

The label "multiculturalism" is first used as a "politically correct" way to designate a number of different movements, such as those related to multi-ethnicity, nationalist claims, certain sexual options, gender issues and, in general, phenomena included in the

pp. 73-90. Or the analysis of Charles Taylor, *Multiculturalism and the Politics of Recognition*, Princeton, NJ, Princeton University Press, 1992. *Id.* "The Politics of Recognition," in A. Gutmann (ed.), *Multiculturalism*, Princeton, NJ, 1994.

3 For an examination of both these terms, see the work of José Rubio-Carracedo, "Pluralismo, multiculturalismo y ciudadanía compleja," in Pablo Badillo O'Farrell (coord.), *Pluralismo, tolerancia, multiculturalismo. Reflexiones para un mundo plural*, Madrid, AKAL-Universidad Internacional de Andalucía, 2003, pp. 173-195. Also see, John Kekes, *The Morality of Pluralism*, Princeton, NJ, Princeton University Press, 1993.

4 Joaquín Abellán, "Los retos del multiculturalismo para el Estado moderno," in Pablo Badillo O'Farrell (coord.), *Pluralismo, tolerancia, multiculturalismo…*, *op. cit.*, pp. 13-33.

term *culture* (understood in the broadest sense). The main supporters of multiculturalism are the *Marxist* theorists that seek the recognition of minority groups within the current societal struggle that exists between diverse and heterogeneous groups. These theorists also reject the neutral stance of the state, proposing active state intervention, which would sometimes lead to the practice of affirmative action that multiculturalists argue for. The concept of multiculturalism is also linked to some *liberal* attempts to respond to cultural diversity, such as those by Isaiah Berlin,[5] John Rawls,[6] Joseph Raz,[7] or Will Kymlicka.[8] In relation to this problem of mul-

5 For writings about Isaiah Berlin, see Ronald M. Dworkin (*et al.*) (eds.), *The Legacy of Isaiah Berlin*, New York, New York Review of Books, 2001.

6 A classic of the recently deceased thinker of Harvard University (1921-2002), his work *Political Liberalism*, New York, Columbia University Press, 2005.

7 From this author, among his various works, the most important regarding this theme are: Joseph Raz, *The Morality of Freedom*, Oxford, Oxford University Press, 1986. *Id. Ethics in the Public Domain: Essays in the Morality of Law and Politics*, Oxford, Clarendon Press; New York, Oxford University Press, 1994.

8 From this author, see, Will Kymlicka (ed.), *The Rights of Minority Cultures*, Oxford, Oxford University Press, 1995. *Id. Ciudadanía multicultural. Una teoría liberal de los derechos de las minorías*, Barcelona-Buenos Aires-México, Paidós, 1996. *Id. Finding Our Way. Rethinking Ethnocultural Relations in Canada*, Toronto, New York, Oxford University Press, 1998. See also concerning the topic, the work of Amartya Kumar Sen, "Democracia y desarrollo. Derechos del hombre y diferencias culturales," Spanish translation by José Iturmendi Morales, in *Anuario de Derechos Humanos, Nueva Época*, Instituto de Derechos Humanos, Universidad Complutense de Madrid, vol. 1, 2000, pp. 367-387, in which the author discusses the contrasts and contradictions between cultures or within the same culture, especially within the North American context and to a lesser extent in the context of Asian and Mulsim cultures. The author highlights the existing relationship between human rights and multiculturalism when he affirms, p. 369, that from this perspective, the concept of the universal rights of man exercises the function of a unifying or integrating idea, that manifests itself in two ways that, at the same time, end up being complementary:

ticulturalism is the concept of "constitutional patriotism." This idea was devised in the 1980s in Germany and later became wide-spread due to the work of the German thinker from the School of Frankfurt, Jürgen Habermas. Habermas wrote of Sternberger's proposal that the love for one's country is synthesized in essence into the love for the established values of the *Rechtsstaat*, written in the context of a split between the Federal Republic of Germany and the Democratic Republic of Germany, which divided the nation. In this setting, constitutional patriotism meant a unifying issue for the citizens of the Federal Republic regarding the values established by the Fundamental Law of Bonn—which is to say, with respect to constitutional values, as opposed to the notion of a national German conscience based on historical and cultural ties. Thus, this sort of patriotism went beyond the idea of simply belonging to a cultural community. In short, constitutional patriotism gives priority to constitutional values over cultural values. This is a marked difference from multiculturalism, which supports public recognition of the different roles played by different cultures.[9]

But in reality, what is multiculturalism as a contemporary phenomenon? It is important to remember that this idea has at least two dimensions. On the one hand, concerning *individuals*, multiculturalism is opposed to any type of social and political discrimination based on cultural differences. On the other hand, however, concerning *groups*, multiculturalism is against assimilationism and instead supports self-determination for different social groups in their most diverse formulations (e.g. homosexuals, feminists, en-

---

a) on one hand the idea provides an element that converts all human people into beings that are the object of a certain distinction or acknowledgement of rank or dignity as said human beings (regardless of their place of residence, or the country of which they are nationals)

b) and on the other hand offers an attribute that all human people share with the rest of human people—shared property that extends to the well-known concept of diversity, which in fact introduces the distinct positivistic legal systems of our respective countries.

9 Pablo Badillo O'Farrell, "¿Pluralismo versus multiculturalismo?", in *Id.* (coord.), *Pluralismo, tolerancia, multiculturalismo..., op. cit.*, pp. 33-67.

vironmentalists, religious communities of the indigenous populations in Canada and Australia, or the Kurds and other national minorities, Muslims and other religious minorities in India, African-Americans in the U.S., etc.). Standing in contrast to assimilationism and the dissolution of the specific traits of the immigrant sectors is the idea of the "melting pot"—a term coined by the Jewish-American writer Israel Zangwill as the title of a play, to describe the mixing of immigrant cultures in the U.S. From this perspective multiculturalism reveals itself as a supporter of the equal treatment of all the groups, also securing (in a second aspect) the survival of the distinct cultures.

From these issues emerges the issue of what one understands as *culture*. First of all, it is clearly a dynamic concept. It is a system of beliefs and practices subject to change over time. Furthermore, it deals with a notion that encompasses varying levels and that includes sectors as disparate as those of linguistics, the maxims and proverbs of popular wisdom, music, literature or art, and lest we forget the legal realm, particularly expressed through the practice of customs.

Multiculturalism enters in conflict with and presents a challenge to the modern *state* and its traditional pillars—knowledge, sovereignty, territorial unity and cultural integrity. As a result, following the Marxist tradition, it becomes apparent that the state is not a necessary entity, and is instead an artificial creation—a superstructure that maintains the tyranny of the dominating classes in power, ruling over the subjugated minorities as they please. Instead of a state structure, multiculturalism erects as its central pillar the individual, and the groups in which the individual integrates, regardless of the type of group. Rather than speak only of a single nation, it tries to define the modern state as comprised of various communities. In such a formulation, the standardized concept of sovereignty enters in crisis, moving towards a society without a single core, as opposed to traditional societies bound by a subsystem—following the terminology of Niklas Luhmann's systemic theory—whether it be science, the economy, education, the family or any other subsystem.

1.2 Multicultural Education as the Opposite of "Ethnocentric" Education. Tolerance as a Key Concept

It is very important for the subsistence of cultural diversity to incorporate multicultural *education*. In other words, the opposite of an ethnocentric education—that which considers the European civilization as the best, not owing anything to anyone, and denoting in large part a certain level of imperialistic arrogance and contemptuous racism. Instead of this, multiculturalism proposes a *cultural dialogue*, of what some refer to as an *alliance of civilizations*. The result would be to expand the study plans, on the one hand, to include the cultural realities of other places and historical periods, and on the other hand, to include the particulars of the local regions and autonomous communities, running the risk of a lack of coordination that such a plan could entail.[10] In a similar way one can find the movement of "political correctness" applied to this field of study. According to said movement, it would be necessary to use the term African-Americans instead of blacks, etc.

A key concept in all multicultural societies is that of tolerance.[11] It is necessary to tolerate differences not only passively (by accepting that there are those that are not like us) but also actively (by trying to search for understanding and dialogue with other cultures and forms of life, which in the end results in more open-minded people and permits society to grow and improve by accepting others, as foreign as their beliefs may seem to us).

---

10 Regarding this topic, see Jurjo Torres Santomé, *Globalización e interdisciplinariedad: el currículo integrado*, Madrid, Ediciones Morata, 1994; 2nd ed. 1996.

11 A classic with respect to the subject of tolerance is the book by the professor of Princeton University Michael Walzer, *On Toleration*, New Haven, Yale University Press, 1997. Regarding the same topic, another valuable work is that of S. Mendus – D. Edwards, *On toleration*, Oxford, Oxford University Press, 1987.

1.3 The State's Answer: Neutrality or Interventionism?

This type of system would breach the neutral attitude of the state, an attitude more characteristic of 19th century liberalism than of the demands of current societies and social-democratic *Rechtsstaat*. It would not be enough then to guarantee a certain margin of individual freedom without state interference. Instead, it is necessary to intervene and *promote* the necessary conditions for liberty and equality so that individuals and groups can make such conditions a reality. This would be accomplished through a policy that guarantees the equality of *opportunities*, at least in the beginning, although later everyone, by virtue of his/her talent, effort, and (yes, why not!) luck, reaches new heights of social and economic comfort.[12]

This interventionist policy would sometimes allow the practice of *affirmative action*—a kind of positive discrimination that would be permissible. Said practice would involve resolving the natural inequalities that exist from birth.[13] Jean-Jacques Rousseau begins

12 This concept works in relation to what Ronald M. Dworkin refers to as the "envy test." This test implies that if every member of Society were asked if he/she agrees with the share of possessions and properties that he/she has been assigned by the "walrasian auction" (named as such in honor of the researcher Leon Walras), equality would exist if nobody was envious of what another person had. This hypothetical auction implies an exercise in trying to bring about an ideal world in a diachronic fashion—throughout personal history as well as throughout the history of Humanity. Thus, Dworkin argues that if a subject X is asked if he is envious of another subject Y, a negative response from X should refer not only to the current moment (in which Y could have more possessions and more wealth than X), but rather also to the kind of life that Y has had and continues having, as compared to that of X, which has allowed Y to arrive at his/her current social standing: all the years dedicated to personal training/education, sacrifices in terms of free-time such as resting and being with family,...

13 Regarding this topic, *vid.* the thought-provoking reflections of Professor José Iturmendi Morales referring to the deaf community, "En torno a la '*Comunidad Sorda*' como comunidad de aprendizaje y de prácticas de pertenencia y de fidelidad. Una aportación al debate entre comunitaristas y liberales acerca de los derechos, los valores y la Sociedad," in

his most emblematic work, *Le contrat social*, claiming that man is born free, but that despite this he finds himself chained everywhere he goes. But how can we speak of liberty if the strong subjugate the weak as they please? Perhaps this apparent contradiction makes more sense if we consider that Rousseau speaks of birth in relation to the French word *nature*, more than in relation to *naissance*, the term which is normally translated to mean birth. Whatever the case, it is undeniable that nature endows the created beings with a series of abilities, capabilities and faculties that largely vary among different individuals: some are born with talent and fortune, while others are born timid and destitute. It is in these cases where the state must *lend a hand* to nature, to avoid that these natural inequalities become impossible to overcome. One of the ways to do so is by utilizing affirmative action, a type of positive discrimination. Discrimination should be referred to in a negative or pejorative manner when the term refers to giving favor and privilege to a certain group without justification. However, when discrimination serves to compensate a natural inequality, it should not be viewed in such a negative manner. If we think about the current situation of affirmative action for women in some areas, we see that it can help reconcile their difficult situation of balancing their family and work life. Although professional women are highly qualified and it appears that their situation in the workplace is changing, it is still evident that the responsibility of motherhood and caring for children has forced many women to settle for less important and worse-paid jobs than their male counterparts.

José Gabriel Storch de Gracia y Asensio (comp.), *Estatuto jurídico de las lenguas de señas en el Derecho español. Aproximaciones*, Madrid, Editorial Universitaria Ramón Areces, 2005, Lesson 1, pp. 3-227, especially in epigraph 1.1.5, which has as it's title, "El principio de igualdad de oportunidades y el tratamiento de las discapacidades," esp. p. 33: "*..., being so universally accepted the idea-force of providing the same opportunities for everyone, it is difficult to impose and materialize said idea up until the final consequences which, in the case of the most underprivileged, requires, for the sake of true and effective equalization ,that an equality of results is made possible—a compensatory education (a higher, more intense level of education for the worst stragglers).*

1.4 *The Value of Conflict*

Before I referred to the term tolerance. This term, however, does not imply that conflict should totally disappear. Conflicts are inevitable and, as such, we have to learn to live with them. The same occurs in psychology with traumas—they cannot be avoided, but they can be resolved. And the best way to do so is not by denying the existence of such problems, but rather by initially admitting their presence and then overcoming the problems. It is important not to assume that conflicts must always necessarily be resolved. The search for a solution is an ethnocentrically puritan concept. The majority of people cling to this idea that conflicts must be resolved. A positive step forward, although only a small one, would be to speak of *conflict management.* Conflicts can be resolved, but we can also learn to live with them. A larger step in the right direction would be to speak of being *concerned with the conflict. Participation in the conflict* would perhaps be the most appropriate term, since it puts the emphasis on the simple act of dealing with the problem instead of on the result of such action.

1.5 *The Clash between Liberalism and Communitarianism. The "Cosmopolitan" Alternative*

The current clash in Philosophy between two opposing schools of thought is a well known one: Liberalism and Communitarianism, which is nothing more than the dilemma between giving priority to the individual characteristics of the *me* or participating as a member of a *group*, whether it be a community or a collective.[14] In

14 Regarding this topic, see Ramón Soriano, *Interculturalismo. Entre Liberalismo y Comunitarismo*, Córdoba, Almuzara, 2004. In this book—esp. pp. 81-151—the author establishes an alternative to the two principal conceptions. According to one such conception, cultures clash in a complex world and exist according to the tradition of a superior culture (that of the West) to which all others would have to conform, in such a way that would reproduce the classic confrontation between civilization and savagery. According to the other main conception, that of the multiculturalists, all cultures have their own rights, and nobody coming

contrast to these opposing schools of thought we can speak of what Jeremy Waldron, among others, described as the *cosmopolitan alternative*.[15]

Cosmopolitanism is partly the result of globalization, but reducing it only to this aspect would perhaps be excessively simplistic, since the idea implies much more.[16] It implies an *education* with a breadth of aims that fall outside the walls of the community itself and that consider the student as a kind of citizen of the world. The concept entails the idea of the passage from the *polis* to the *cosmopolis*, to the planetary village, with all the aspects that such a notion implies. Thus, nowadays it is common to be born in one place, to later study in another, to change your place of residence several times during your life (e.g. for work reasons), to love the cuisine of different countries, to enjoy the music from other cultures, and so on in many aspects of one's life. Partitions, barriers and borders are

---

from outside their culture should be able to interfere with their system of rights. The group itself should be the basic subject of said rights, and as such within any country there could exist as many systems of rights as there are cultural groups in the state.

Not fully agreeing with this latter conception, Ramón Soriano defends a new thesis, which consists of starting up intercultural dialogue in which both the liberals (clinging to their conception of universal principles exportable to all cultures) and the communitarians (who are overly-attached to the peculiarities of local communities) can participate. Interculturalism would open the door to a third, alternative conception that lies between liberalism and communitarianism. The book examines the theories of liberal thinkers such as John Rawls, Will Kymlicka, Joseph Raz and Jürgen Habermas, as well as communitarian thinkers such as Charles Taylor and Michael Walzer.

15 Jeremy Waldron, "Minority Cultures and the Cosmopolitan Alternative." in Will Kymlicka (ed.), *The Rights of Minority Cultures, op. cit.*, pp. 93-119.

16 Regarding this topic, see Mikhaël Elbaz - Dense Helly (dirs.), *Globalización, ciudadanía y multiculturalismo,* proface to the Spanish edition of Enrique E. Raya Lozano, Granada, Maristán, 2002. Javier de Lucas, *Globalización e identidades: claves políticas y jurídicas,* Barcelona, Icaria, 1rst ed., 2003. Javier de Lucas (*et al.*), *La multiculturalidad,* Madrid, Consejo General del Poder Judicial, 1st ed., 1st reprint, 2002.

all broken down, and in the process the field of vision continues to expand.

It is also relevant to point out that Religion (as a phenomenon of universalization) is currently experiencing a resurgence or *revival*, despite Nietzsche's prediction that advocated its disappearance: "God is dead." God is not dead. Nietzsche, however, is.

1.6 Individual Rights and Collective Rights. Respect for Minorities

The central core of classic liberal human rights declarations is traditionally composed of individual rights—the first generation rights, such as civil and political rights. However, with the passage of time and the consolidation of the social welfare state and later of the social and democratic state , the emphasis has been placed on collective rights—the second generation rights, such as economic, social and cultural rights. What's more, in the third generation rights (some even speak of the existence of a fourth generation), in relation with the ideas of cosmopolitism and globalization, the active subject of human rights is a category that is continually expanding. As such, the discourse surrounding these third generation rights is related to the right of nations to self-determination, rights that belong to all humanity, or to society as a whole. With respect to the passive holder of such rights, the subject responsible for their implementation, we also see an expanding category: ranging from the state to supranational organizations such as the United Nations, creating at the same time international criminal jurisdiction with the International Criminal Court.

But, at the same time, rights organized in this fashion produce minority groups that, due to their minority status, have a difficult time being heard in a democracy where the rule of the majorities dominates and the decision making is done by these majorities. Despite this, minorities must not be forgotten. Henry David Thoreau, the father of civil disobedience, indicates that a minority of one with more sense than his/her fellow citizens is actually a majority of one. When such a person doesn't comply with the majority's orders and instead resists them with all his/her might, said person is unstoppable. Multiculturalism has much to do with the existence of such minority groups in a democracy—with the coexistence of a plurality of cultures whose demands deserve a response.

1.7 Pluralism

Pluralism is a moral conception regarding the respect for foreign beliefs,[17] according to which there is *no such a thing as an absolute truth* capable of prevailing in all cultures, valid in all time periods and places in the same manner.

In contrast to the idea of *a priori* truths, sometimes derived (classic natural law) from the idea of nature, other times (medieval natural law) from divinity, and in other instances (rationalist natural law) from reason, or from an autocratic leader (in whom the community places its trust and to whom it gives the reigns of power, especially in times of crisis), the fact remains that many times *the* truth is nothing more than the sum of all the present individual *truths*. Although it is reasonable to admit, paraphrasing George Orwell's famous description in the satire *Animal Farm*, that "*we are all equal, but there are some who are more equal than other*," or that *justice is an arguable value, but there are things that are objectively more just than others*, one could also affirm that *there are no absolute truths, but there are truths that are truer than others*. Recognizing the relative value of the truth must not bring about skepticism or a belief in relativism. It is necessary to make use of doubt—the type of methodical doubt that Descartes speaks of—as a means to free us from our useless prejudices. This philosophy is made clear by classical thinkers with the phrases "*omnibus est dubitandum*" (one must doubt everything), "*sapere aude*" (dare to know). But the conclusion we reach cannot be, or at least should not be, the doubt itself. Some dogmatic convictions should come to our aid and help

17 Dealing with the philosophical basis of pluralism, see the work of José M. Sevilla, "Algunas raíces filosóficas del pluralismo en la modernidad," in Pablo Badillo O'Farrell (comp.), *Pluralismo, tolerancia, multiculturalismo...*, op. cit., pp. 195-233.

us live—for we must not forget that "there are some things that are truer than others."

The notion of pluralism tells us that it is erroneous to consider those that think like us as friends and those that think in a different way as enemies or that the world is divided between good and evil. In other words, it is a false notion to believe that everything is either black or white, because in reality what dominates in life are shades of gray—we are all sometimes good, and sometimes less good. Going against the Greek and Roman ideology that those who did not speak their language and who lived outside their respective borders were *barbarians*, against the Catholic Orthodox doctrine of considering all those who did not strictly follow the religion in its pure form as *heretics*, against the conviction of institutions like the Inquisition that if you deviated from the rules the solution was to burn you at the stake, against the Ancien Regime's maxim that you were not part of humanity unless you were at least a baron, exists the democratic theory. Said theory has at its core the notion of "*one man, one vote*," which permits the possibility of dissenting and expressing other viewpoints (even ones that go against the majority), as long as the *rules of the game* are respected—the rules of the democratic game such as freedom of speech, pluralism and tolerance.[18]

18 Regarding this topic, see G. MacLennan, *Pluralism*, London, Open University Press, 1995. An example of pluralism and tolerance according to many people, that has been proven and demonstrated, is the case of Al-Ándalus, in the coexistence of Christians, Moors and Jews, where no governing power was interested in physically eliminating people who followed a religion that differed from the official one, nor in giving the ultimatum of convert or die. This opinion, however, is put in doubt by González Jiménez, in "El problema de la tolerancia en la España de las tres culturas," in Pablo Badillo O'Farrell (coord.), *Pluralismo, tolerancia, multiculturalismo…, op. cit.*, pp. 125-141, in which the author points out that the fact that the Quran contains clear references to tolerance, should not cause us to forget that in the beginning Islam was propagated in large part by the sword. Furthermore, in Al-Ándalus we witness the introduction of the "yizya," or the "price of faith"—a special tax that non-Muslims had to pay in order to receive the society's tolerance. Also containing interesting material on the topic, in the same volume, is an article by

1.8 *The Classification of Moral Temperaments*

In this discussion involving notions of morality, it is helpful to examine the typology of moral temperaments outlined by Agustín Squella Narducci.[19] According to Squella Narducci the moral temperaments would be, by order of least to most radical, the following: indifference, neutrality, relativism, skepticism, fallibility, absolutism and fanaticism.[20]

First of all would be the *indifferent* person, who does *not have a moral opinion*. Such a person remains in the plain of the morally indescribable, which is neither a good nor a bad thing. In a way those who are indifferent are people that live with less intensity than others. It would be somewhat similar to vegetating or living in a greenhouse, in a type of bubble, which isolates such people from the mortal world—a world which often requires one to commit oneself to something. This is the position of some intellectuals who prefer to remain in their ivory tower instead of getting involved in current problems. It is true, in a sense, the opinion of those that claim there are two molds of people: those that act and those that watch—the actors and the spectators. Although it is difficult to find a person who merely plays the role of spectator, since as we become adults we must opt for certain paths (choosing a job, whether to get mar-

---

the diplomat Alfonso López Perona, "Tres experiencias pluriculturales: India, EEUU, Peru," pp. 143-171, in which he narrates his personal experiences in said countries.

19 These classifications were outlined in his address to the World Congress of Legal Philosophy which took place from the 10th to the 15th of August, 1997 in the cities of Buenos Aires and La Plata. A short time before said presentation, this typology appeared in an article by the same author published in the *Revista de Ciencias Sociales de la Universidad de Valparaiso (Chile).*

20 Regarding this topic, see Fernando Falcón y Tella, *Tridimensionalismo y Derecho,* Madrid, Servicio de Publicaciones, Facultad de Derecho, Universidad Complutense de Madrid, 2004, pp. 135-139. Reviewed by Professor Juan Antonio Martínez Muñoz, in *Foro, Revista de Ciencias Jurídicas y Sociales, Facultad de Derecho, Universidad Complutense de Madrid,* 0/2004, pp. 317-320.

ried, where to live, etc.) that exclude other options, it still remains true that there are many degrees of commitment.

After the indifferent person, comes the *neutral* person, who *has a moral opinion, but does not show it.* In this category we find those who prefer not to express their opinions, for a diverse range of reasons. They prefer simple comfort and do not wish to look for problems by making commitments. People of this mold often are slightly cowardly individuals that, although they have an opinion, do not descend into the political, social, or cultural arena to defend it.

In the third position is the *relativist,* who *has a moral opinion, shows it, but recognizes that it is not better than everyone else's opinions.* This is a stance that requires only a bit more commitment than the others. Far from considering him/herself as the exclusive and absolute holder of the truth, the relativist is humble in his/her own self-appraisal. For me this stance is especially likeable and is very common among people with a high level of intelligence and education. The more one knows, the more one realizes what they still have not learned. Fanaticism—believing that you are in possession of total truth and that this truth is the only one—is clearly a reductionist stance. Wanting to understand the universe is like trying to fit all the water in the ocean into a hole in the sand on the beach. If you were to try to do so alone, or even with the help of all Humanity, it would still be futile. Just as the hole in the sand is very small in comparison to the entire ocean, so too is the history of human life miniscule in comparison with the existence of the universe. Thus, it is impossible to actually be the holder of absolute truth as the fanatics claim.

After the relativist comes the *skeptic,* which is to say someone who *has a moral opinion, shows it, thinks it is better than everyone else's opinions, but admits that it is not possible to demonstrate this.* This stance perhaps suffers a bit of laziness, of giving in too easily. If someone is actually in conditions to affirm that his/her truth is the best, there is no reason why such a person should not be able demonstrate it, or at the very least attempt to do so and fight for his/her point of view.

Next we have the *fallible* person, or the subject who *has a moral opinion, shows it, recognizes that it is better than everyone else's opinions and that this can be demonstrated, but believes that he/she can still learn from others.* In my opinion, this is a very wise position. Although it may be true that we are in possession of a true result, this result will only really be one truth, our truth, at the service of a broader truth, of "*the*" truth, if such a thing exists. In this way one can also point out that education focused solely on memorization is just as bad as education that does not have in mind the lessons of the past. When students complain about the excess of repetition and memorization that is required of them to pass different subjects, one must remember that education is not only teaching to think (although this is one part of education) but rather teaching thoughts (which are an important part of the tradition of education). If the man of every generation starts from scratch, he will lose the opportunity to learn from the errors and (why not!) successes of the past.[21]

A still more radical posture is that of the *absolutist*, the person who *has a moral opinion, shows it, recognizes that it is better than everyone else's opinion and that this can be demonstrated, and considers that there is nothing he/she can learn from someone else, but that others have something to learn from him/her.* The truth is that in life there are very few absolutes. How do trees fall more easily with the wind? Which are the trees that are most resistant—those with a flexible trunk or those with hard bark, that oppose greater resistance? Being inflexible leads to headaches and doesn't allow us to develop our life in many aspects. However, we should not view a minimum of certainty as something negative. It is true that having doubts about any matter is a good method of investigation, but we cannot doubt everything forever: doubts can be the starting point and method, but the goal, the result of our inquiry, should contain a minimum of legal security, a certain knowledge that we should stick to. At the service of this certainty is the law, for instance.

---

21 Hans Kelsen: "Absolutismo y relativismo en Filosofía y en Política," in *Qué es Justicia*, pp. 113-125.

Finally, the most extreme position is situated with that of the *fanatic*, such an individual who *has a moral opinion, shows it, thinks it is better than everyone else's opinion and that this can be demonstrated, but considers that there is nothing he/she can learn from everyone else and that it is not necessary to try to convince them, but rather that what we should do is eliminate them.* This stance is not very advisable. It is possible to attribute some of the greatest errors and horrors of the past century and part of the evils present today to those who have taken such a stance. I am thinking particularly about the wars, especially the fratricidal ones that come about due to nationalism. Terrorism also comes to mind—when through terror it is attempted to impose beliefs or ideas which should, for their own essence, be free. Not even religious wars are free of the plague of death and desolation that all war conflicts entail. This was the case of the crusades, the so-called "holy war," and in the modern crusade against evil, which is not justified with the traditional idea of legitimate defense, but rather hoists the "preventative" flag of war.

Having now seen the classification of moral temperaments, the thesis defended is that skepticism makes us more tolerant and helps the securing of axiological pluralism.[22] As such, Isaiah Berlin establishes a connection between evaluative pluralism (moral skepticism) and political pluralism (based on the priority of the values of tolerance and liberty) and, on the contrary, between moral universalism (evaluative monism) and authoritarianism and political totalitarianism.

1.9 The Mass Media as a Manipulator of Public Opinion, as Opposed to Pluralism and Respect for Minorities

Pluralism, as we have understood it, is incompatible with a system that controls and manipulates public opinion. Our ideas of reality often do not exactly correspond to reality itself, but rather they are

22 This is the opinion, for example, of Elena García Guitián, "La repercusión política del pluralismo valorativo," in Pablo Badillo O'Farrell (coord.), *Pluralismo, tolerancia, multiculturalismo…*, *op. cit.*, pp. 107-125.

influenced by what the media broadcasts. Thus, one could distinguish between the "real reality" (the redundancy is useful here) and a "virtual reality," which is what we encounter once information has passed through the sieve that is the media: the written press, radio, and especially television and films. These types of media often utilize a subtle and deliberate manipulation of reality, which results in the distortion of said reality. To begin with, it is the media that selects which matters it will focus its interest on as well as that of the public's, leaving aside other topics which it does not find "convenient" to deal with at the time. The most important topics, those that could put governments and political parties in check, are never debated. Furthermore, television, for instance, not only not broadcasts "excessively embarrassing" topics (in reality the opposite), but rather it also analyzes and interprets the topics that it broadcasts and tells us what we should think about them and how we must interpret and understand them. As a result, this method becomes the most effective form of propaganda and manipulation ever employed. And what can we say about private television channels, which more than informing the viewer, have as their goal making the people who control their station wealthier?

What sense would it make to speak of pluralism in this context? What would be the value in this setting of minority opinions? If, contrary to the belief of stoics, Cicero and the Christians, the human social order is not natural but rather cognitive—which is to say that it is the consequence of a long learning process—that means that what we think is the consequence of a learning process. If this process was erroneous or the result of the cultural context and influence of the mass media, the feeling of democratic plurality would be just that, a feeling, an appearance, that in reality would hide powerful class, economic, and political interests. The situation becomes even more complicated with the expansion of new technologies, which strengthen the alliance between power and the media.[23]

23 This analysis is covered well in Enrique Bocardo Crespo, "Los asaltos al pluralismo," in Pablo Badillo O'Farrell (comp.), *Pluralismo, tolerancia, multiculturalismo…, op. cit.*, pp. 67-107.

2 The International Criminal Court

2.1 *Precedents*

2.1.1 Before World War II

The desire to create a venue to prosecute people suspected of committing crimes at an international level and then sanctioning such people if found guilty dates back quite some time. Such a hope almost became a reality after World War I when, on the basis of the compromise solution of the 1919 Versailles Treaty regarding the punishment of people involved in the war, a special tribunal was established to judge the German Kaiser Wilhelm II for committing a crime that went against the moral norms of the international community. This initiative, however, did not work out in the end because the Netherlands (where the Kaiser was taking refuge) did not want to turn the Kaiser over to the Allies because they considered his actions nothing more than a "political crime" and as such deserving of a kind of "extenuating treatment" with regards to his punishment. Nonetheless, for the first time a head of state was considered personally responsible for his illegal polices against the most basic norms and principles of international law.[24]

The notion of creating an international criminal justice system reappeared in the interwar period by the International Law Association. In its thirty fourth conference, which took place in Vienna in 1926, the members argued about the idea of creating an inter-

24 Regarding this topic, see, among others, Juan Francisco Escudero Espinosa, *La Corte Penal Internacional y el Consejo de Seguridad. Hacia la paz por la Justicia*, Madrid, Diles, 2004, esp. pp. 39-43. Isabela Martins García Leite, *Tribunal Penal Internacional como una contribución real a la paz y a la seguridad de la humanidad en el ámbito de la Organización de las Naciones Unidas*, specialization dissertation, Instituto de Derechos Humanos, Facultad de Derecho, Universidad Complutense de Madrid, directed by Manuel Pérez González, 1997, unpublished, esp. pp. 4-26. See also, Deysi Yolima Porras Leal, *La creación de la Corte Penal Internacional*, specialization dissertation, Instituto de Derechos Humanos, Facultad de Derecho, Universidad Complutense de Madrid, directed by Manuel Pérez González, 1999, unpublished, esp. pp. 22-65.

national criminal court and also about what crimes should be included as part of said court's jurisdiction. As a result, in the thirty ninth conference, which took place in Paris in 1936, the members of the Association passed a Declaration in which they established that the Permanent Court of International Justice would have jurisdiction over all violations of the "General treaty of 1928 condemning recourse to war for the solution of international controversies" (referring to the Kellogg-Briand Pact). The results were not, however, what were hoped for.

But it was in 1937 when perhaps the most serious and specific attempt was made to establish an international criminal court. This occurred with the Convention for the Prevention and Punishment of Terrorism, which ordered the establishment of an international criminal court to prosecute acts of terrorism. In the end the proposal also became a failure, since it did not achieve ratification by the number of states necessary.

2.1.2 After World War II

A *The International Military Tribunals of Nuremberg and Tokyo*

a General Considerations

World War II (1939-1945) and the terrible crimes perpetrated in its midst, especially by the Nazis, caused a strong resurgence in the conviction that it was necessary to punish those who were guilty of such atrocious acts and to establish international justice that would be even more significant and important than the horrors lived out during the war. How could it be conceivable not to prosecute those that had started the war and committed such appalling crimes in the conflict? It was the Allies' idea, expressed in their Moscow Declaration on October 30, 1943. As a result, on August 8, 1945, the London Charter created the first International Military Tribunal in history, that of Nuremberg, to prosecute the most important war criminals of Europe. Said jurisdiction also corresponded in Asia to the International Tribunal of Tokyo (1946). In addition to these two international military tribunals, the only ones that existed at that time, Ordinance number 10 of the Control Council, on December 20, 1945, laid out the creation of Military Tribunals by the Allies in their respective areas of occupation to judge lower-ranking officials.

Regarding general considerations related to the Nuremberg and Tokyo proceedings, one can point out that in the first place neither the principle of neutrality nor the principle of legality ("*nullum crimen nulla poena sine praevia lege poenale*") were present in the prosecution of crimes against humanity. Also regarding crimes against humanity, the prohibition of retroactively applied criminal laws (which does not allow incriminating *ex post facto* laws) was ignored. The response to these critiques was to argue that crimes against peace had already been established before, in the ban on wars of aggression put forth in the Kellogg-Briand Pact, as well as in the Hague Conventions and in the very penal codes and international military laws of the countries involved in the war. Even more problematic was the justification of the sanction against crimes against humanity, crimes which appeared for the first time in the Nuremberg Statute. Most of the problems and criticisms arising from Nuremberg were attributed to a judge from the United States Supreme Court, and chief prosecutor for his country in the trials, H. Jackson. Jackson also personally prepared the project of the Tribunal's statute. When the first trial ended he resigned from his position as chief prosecutor for the U.S. due to the aforementioned criticism that he suffered in that role.

b The Nuremberg International Military Tribunal

The governments of the victors of World War II—the United States, the United Kingdom and Northern Ireland, the U.S.S.R., and France (in other words the allied countries)- signed an agreement for the creation of the Nuremberg Tribunal, whose constitution, jurisdiction and competence was established in the London Charter on August 8, 1945. The establishment of the Nuremberg Tribunal was attached to the London Charter in the following manner:

- In the *composition* of the Tribunal the only countries that intervened were the four powers that were victorious in the great conflict. Each of these countries was able to designate one of the four members of the Tribunal—judges Biddle (U.S.) and Lawrence (United Kingdom), who presided over the hearings,

General Nikinchenko (U.S.S.R.) and Professor Donnedieu de Vabres (France)—none of whom could be challenged. As a result the Tribunal was disapproved of for incorporating a "victor's justice" on a functional and organic level. In 403 sessions, all public (which took place between November 10, 1945 and August 31, 1946) twenty one important war criminals were tried, out of which twelve received the death penalty in a sentence delivered on October 1, 1946.

– With regards to the *procedure*, the Tribunal's Statute contemplated certain guarantees for the accused—especially with respect to the publicizing of the process, translations and defense. At the same time, however, the Statute admitted the possibility of trying and condemning the accused in default or in absentia (art. 12 of the Statute). It also did not totally respect the principle of being able to argue all decisions before the court, since in the final subsection of art. 10 it is stated that "the criminal nature of the group or organization is considered proved and *shall not be questioned.*" The Statute also infringed on the legal prohibition of being accused of the same crime twice by different courts, since art. 11 of the Statute allows for independent or additional criminal charges to be brought against someone who has already been convicted by the Nuremberg Tribunal. Such charges could be brought against a person already convicted at Nuremberg by another criminal court—whether it be a national court, a military court, or a court established by occupying forces.
– In terms of the *"ratione materiae" competence* of the Tribunal, art. 6, sections a) and d), of the Statute, establish four charges that the court has jurisdiction over. The first was the *common plan or conspiracy.* The second was *crimes against peace,* which take place when in the process of *jus ad bellum,* a war of aggression or a war in violation of the treaties is unjustifiably unleashed. Third were *war crimes strictly speaking,* which are committed during hostilities when violations of *jus in bello* occur. Despite the saying "all is fair in love and war," at least in the latter it is necessary to follow certain rules at the time of executing such a war. Finally, the Tribunal had jurisdiction

over *crimes against humanity*, which are crimes that threaten life, integrity or individual or collective human rights.

One could mention as the principles of the Nuremberg Statute the following:

1 The *rejection of immunity for heads of state.*
2 The *rejection of due obedience* (i.e. following the orders of your government or a hierarchical superior) *as grounds for exemption from guilt.* For the first time in history the right to disobey an unjust order or law was transformed from a moral right to a moral duty, and also a legal one, by implementing a corresponding punishment or criminal sanction against those who obeyed unjust laws. Although due obedience was not considered as grounds for exemption in the Nuremberg trials, it was an issue that could be used to soften the court's punishment of the accused.
3 *Individual responsibility* derived from international legal obligations was another principle that was followed. In accordance with this principle, actual persons were tried by the war crimes commission, and not organizations or states as abstract entities. When it was a situation that dealt with organizations, the members themselves were identified and individually tried. In fact, the Nuremberg proceedings gave a significant push to the evolution of international law, because it extended its application to the actions of individuals, holding individuals directly accountable before international society, and not just before limited state jurisdiction. Since Nuremberg the subject of international law is not only the state, but rather also the individual, who is considered as a member of an inter-state society.

c The Tokyo International Military Tribunal

The so-called Far East Military Tribunal, with its headquarters in Tokyo, was created by the proclamation of an American general of the area, Douglas MacArthur. Its sessions began on June, 1946 and tried 28 people, of which seven were condemned to death and the rest to jail sentences in the sentence pronounced on November 12, 1948.

The Tribunal was formed by eleven members, including those of the four great powers as well as others from countries with belligerent attitudes towards Japan (Australia, Canada, China, the Philippines, Holland and New Zealand). India was also included as a neutral participant, in order to avoid criticism of unilateral action and bias. With respect to its jurisdiction, the confusing figure of the "common plan or conspiracy" referenced in the Nuremberg Statute was eliminated. As such, the Tribunal only had jurisdiction over crimes against peace, war crimes, and crimes against humanity. The rulings could be appealed before the United States Supreme Court, and such appeals did take place, although in the end none of the appeals were actually victorious.

Aside from the proceedings in Tokyo, the U.S. also established military commissions in the Philippines to judge Japanese officials for war crimes. The only proceedings against an allied power for war crimes during World War II was brought by Japanese citizens (Shimoda) against the United States for the dropping of the atomic bombs at Hiroshima and Nagasaki, as an infraction of the customs and laws of war. The Japanese Supreme Court, however, rejected the case for jurisdictional reasons in December, 1963.

B The Ad Hoc *International Criminal Tribunals for the Ex-Yugoslavia and Rwanda*

At the end of the cold War, the Security Council, revitalized after its earlier *de facto* inoperative character, created with its Resolutions 827 (from May 25, 1993) and 955 (from November 8, 1994) two international criminal tribunals with the exclusive purpose of trying those charged with being responsible for the serious massive and widespread violations of international humanitarian law (*personal jurisdiction*) which took place in the Ex-Yugoslavia, especially in Bosnia-Herzegovina (*territorial jurisdiction*), beginning on January 1, 1991 and ending on a date to be established by the Security Council which would determine when peace was finally established (*temporal jurisdiction*). The violations included ethnic purges, assassinations, mass murder, rape, looting and destruction of public, cultural and religious property, and arbitrary arrests and detentions (*material jurisdiction*). In addition there was also the crime of genocide ("the killing of members of an ethnic group with the intention of destroying it completely or in part," where *hutu* elements perpetrated the murder of members of the *tutti* group in a concerted, planned and methodic manner with the intention of exterminating the *tutti* completely) in Rwanda and its neighboring states beginning on April 6, 1994—a date on which a plane that carried, among others, the Rwandan Head of State, crashed in Kigali's airport for reasons which are, in theory, unknown—and erupting into an internal conflict that triggered a wave of killings, above all in Kigali. These tribunals did not represent the creation of an international criminal jurisdiction of a permanent nature, but rather were *ad hoc* tribunals, created to judge the specific facts of a particular conflict and of a determined space-time framework.

C The Human Rights Chamber for Bosnia Herzegovina

At the end of the 1990s there were also serious human rights violations that took place in the same geographic areas which had already been shaken by earlier such conflicts—mainly the Balkans and Africa.

The dismemberment of the Yugoslav Socialist Federal Republic gave the hope of autonomy to a range of ethnic groups, which have only partially found a solution with the secession of Slovenia and Croatia. In this tense situation in the interior of Yugoslavia, given the difficulty of a peaceful coexistence, an armed conflict arose in Bosnia Herzegovina which had an "ethnic cleansing" campaign at its core. The Bosnian conflict concluded with the Dayton Accords on December 14, 1995. The Accords include a Framework Agreement and eleven declarations. The sixth declaration formed a Human Rights Chamber and also resulted in the formation of various tribunals for the repression of the international crimes that had been committed. The Chamber has a mixed composition, made up of fourteen judges who were selected among a group of people who were not citizens of Bosnia Herzegovina. Regarding the applicable law, the Human Rights Chamber must judge the human rights violations included in the European Human Rights Convention, its protocols, and in other international treaties, despite the fact that, interestingly enough, these same agreements at the time of the Dayton Accords were not agreed upon and ratified by Bosnia Herzegovina. What's more, it was a judicial organ that was instituted after the illicit acts had been committed, in an *ex post factum* fashion, which goes against the principle of not having laws retroactively applied—an established norm in the criminal justice system. The responsibility of actively legitimizing the proceedings before the Human Rights Chamber, whose decisions are final and are not subject to appeal, lies in the hands of the individuals, non-governmental organizations, and groups of individuals that consider themselves victims of a human rights violation or that can act in the defense of victims who have allegedly died or disappeared.[25]

D The Commission Instituted between Ethiopia and Eritrea

In addition to the Balkans, there have also been other serious human rights violations in Africa. In order to prevent future violations, at the end of the Ethiopia-Eritrea conflict a commission was established in the peace treaty of December 12, 2000. The commission makes binding and final decisions regarding human rights violations, serious violations in international humanitarian law (including those contained in the 1949 Geneva Convention), and violations of international law that took place in said conflict. In order to do so the commission has a *ratione personae* and *ratione loci* jurisdiction, which means that it not only can judge the controversies that arose between the two states in the conflict, but also those violations that relate to the citizens themselves of said states. Only the states, however, and not the physical and legal persons under the states' internal jurisdiction, have the ability to bring about proceedings. Since the commission is also allowed to judge serious human rights violations, in this sense it is similar to the *ad hoc* tribunals instituted for the Ex-Yugoslavia and Rwanda. Less interest arises in the situation of violations of international law, in which case the commission is able to pass judgment. In such a situation the commission acts

25 Angela Del Vecchio, *Giurisdizione internazionale e globalizzazione. I tribunali internazionali tra globalizzazione e frammentazione*, Milano, Giuffrè, 2003, pp. 161-163.

more like an arbitration committee that decides *ex bono et aequo*, which is to say, paying attention to fairness.[26]

E *The Special Court for Sierra Leone*

Along with the conflict between Ethiopia and Eritrea, there were also other serious international crimes that were committed in Africa, such as those perpetrated in the course of the civil war which took place in Sierra Leone in 1991.

In this case, the initiative to create a court that would be able to sanction the most serious crimes committed during the civil war did not come from the agreements that were put into force at the end of the conflict, as was the case of the wars in Bosnia and Ethiopia-Eritrea. Instead, in this case the initiative came from the President of Sierra Leone himself, by virtue of an agreement reached between the United Nations and Sierra Leone at Freetown on January 16, 2002.

Unlike the criminal tribunals for the Ex-Yugoslavia and Rwanda, which were created as subsidiary organs of the Security Council, and were in a way imposed on the states, the Special Court for Sierra Leone was desired by the state and is not an organ of the United Nations. Instead of this, it is a tribunal with its own jurisdiction and a mixed composition, that applies international law and the internal law of Sierra Leone, and that is formed by international judges and judges elected by Sierra Leone.

With regards to *ratione personae* jurisdiction, only those who "bear the greatest responsibility" should be submitted to the court. This responsibility includes the violation of the norms of international humanitarian law or Sierra Leone's internal law—e.g. acts perpetrated by the leaders and military bosses that have threatened the peace with their criminal conduct. Also, an effort was made so that crimes committed by people with a special status like the *peacekeepers* and other personnel present in Sierra Leone during the conflict were not left unpunished. In addition, it was stipulated that minors who were fifteen years old or younger would not be

26 Angela Del Vecchio, *Giurisdizione internazionale e globalizzazione...*, *op. cit.*, pp. 163-164.

judged by the court. The court would also not judge people who in the moment when the crime occurred were between fifteen and eighteen years old, many of whom were submitted to physical or psychological violence, torture, or drugs, which transformed the victims into killers. Minors who were eighteen years old could only be judged if they had committed the most serious of crimes and had served as the ringleader that pushed a group to commit such acts.

With respect to the special court's *ratione materiae* jurisdiction, this jurisdiction allowed the court to judge the most serious violations of international humanitarian law and the laws of Sierra Leone that were perpetrated beginning on November 30, 1996. Regarding the laws of Sierra Leone, it is not a reference to Sierra Leone's entire criminal law code, but rather only to the laws that refer to crimes of child abuse (the *Prevention of Cruelty to Children Act* of 1926) and to those of groundless destruction of property (the *Malicious Damage Act* of 1861), when such acts do not fall within the pursuable categories of international law—in other words, those of a *subsidiary* nature.

It is established that the special court (specifically its appeals chamber) "shall be guided" by the sentences of the appeals chamber that the tribunals for the Ex-Yugoslavia and Rwanda both have. Through this foresight, the court reveals its intention of forming a case law that is as homogenous as possible in the field of international criminal justice. Such case law could serve as a point of reference, whether it be for the International Criminal Court, for domestic tribunals, or in view of possible future crimes.[27]

2.2 Its Creation and Statute

In the 1990s one of the methods that the United Nations used to bring together the international community (governments, non-governmental organizations, representatives of civilian society,

27 Angela Del Vecchio, *Giurisdizione internazionale e globalizzazione...*, *op. cit.*, pp. 164-170. In addition to the above-cited cases, this author also alludes to other *ad hoc* criminal tribunals: those in Cambodia, East Timor and Kosovo. Regarding the topic, see pp. 170-175.

etc.[28]) was the organization of world conferences regarding a topic of particular importance for humanity. One such important conference was the Rome Conference, which officially began on June 15, 1998, with the objective of creating the permanent International Criminal Court that the UN had been trying to establish for fifty years.[29]

At the conference, there were a total of sixty six *like-minded states*, in favor of supporting the Statute for the creation of the court. Of these, thirty three were Western European States, along with which was vitally important the work of many African and Latin American countries and also a scarce representation of certain Islamic countries. Another sector was made up of the *powerful* states, which was formed in part by members of the Security Council, that requested that the intervention of the court be subject to Security Council resolutions. Finally, there was the group of countries that

28 Regarding the topic of the role of international organizations in human rights matters, José Manuel Sánchez Patrón, *Las organizaciones internacionales ante las violaciones de los derechos humanos*, Oviedo, Septem Ediciones, 2004.

29 Regarding the topic, see Nicolás Cabezudo Rodríguez, *La Corte Penal Internacional*, Madrid, Dykinson, 2002. *El Tribunal Penal Internacional*, Barcelona, Revista del Centre d'Estudis Juridics i Formació Espècializtzada, Forum, nº 2, 2003. *El Tribunal Penal Internacional: Mesa redonda organizada por la Asociación de Ex Diputados y Ex Senadores de las Cortes Generales de España, celebrada en Madrid el 29 de junio de 1999*, Madrid, Cortes Generales, 2000. Juan Francisco Escudero Espinosa, *La Corte Penal Internacional y el Consejo de Seguridad: hacia una paz por la justicia*, Madrid, Editorial Diles, 2004. Sergio García Ramírez, *La Corte Penal Internacional*, México, Instituto Nacional de Ciencias Penales, 2002. Juan-Luis Gómez Colomer, *El Tribunal Penal Internacional: investigación y acusación: (un estudio comparado sobre la influencia de modelos y realidades en el tratamiento del principio acusatorio en las fases previas al juicio del proceso penal ante el Tribunal Penal Internacional*, Valencia, Tirant Lo Blanch, 2003. VV.AA., *Hacia una justicia internacional*, Madrid, Ministerio de Justicia, BSCH, Civitas, 2000. Various authors, *La criminalización de la barbarie: la Corte Penal Internacional*, Madrid, Consejo General del Poder Judicial, 2000. J. Quel López (ed.), *Creación de una jurisdicción penal internacional*, Madrid, AEPDIRI / BOE / Escuela Diplomática, 2000, Colección Escuela Diplomática, nº 4.

was *opposed* to the court, formed by the "permanent" members of the Security Council (the United States, France, China and Russia) that advocated an International Criminal Court under the control of the Council and over which the Council could exercise its veto right. Also part of this category of countries opposed to the court was a large sector of Islamic states.

The main obstacle at the Rome Conference was the evident and necessary transfer of sovereignty that the approval of the Court's Statute would entail for the states. There was also opposition and pressure from certain countries that feared that their nationals, and even their leaders and members of their military ranks, could be tried by the Court.

This was the case of the United States, the current world superpower whose largest fear lied in the approval of *automatic* jurisdiction for crimes against humanity and crimes of rape and torture (considered war crimes), since their soldiers could end up being accused of such crimes. The level of tension rose to such a point that even human rights organizations that attended the conference feared that Washington officials would leave the meeting, and with them, the officials of countries that shared the U.S.'s thesis: key countries like India, China, France and Russia. It is not as if these governments did not want to avoid future tragedies like those of Rwanda, Bosnia or Cambodia, but they did insist on an element of cooperation between countries for the possible arrest of criminals. For some, the U.S.'s disagreements did nothing more than confirm a principal characteristic of U.S. foreign policy regarding human rights at a universal level: the U.S.'s tendency to firmly adopt unilateral positions and not limit itself by international instruments. As a result, the U.S. made clear that it would not stay quiet, and that it was necessary to fight against the Rome Treaty and to aggressively oppose the creation of the Court, due to the possible implications that it could have for United States foreign policy.

At the same time, the Chinese government, a fervent defender of national sovereignty, equally feared the creation of the Court, because the situation of oppression maintained in Tibetan territory could without a doubt have become an excellent candidate for the Court's attention.

Finally on July 17, 1998 the Court was formed. Israel's vote against the Court was surprising and generated protests from human rights advocates, who considered it a betrayal to the spirit of Nuremberg and the victims of the Nazi regime during World War II. In the months following the Statute's approval, a process of ratification began. The ratification was open to the signature of all of the states in the Italian Ministry of Foreign Relations. Since October 17, 1998, it passed to the United Nations headquarters in New York, needing the signature of at least sixty states to take effect.

The *characteristics* of the International Criminal Court are:

- Its *independence* (free from the state pressure).
- Its *permanent nature* (unlike the *ad hoc* tribunals created for specific conflicts).
- Its *intention of being universal* (more of an intention than a reality, since it is established that in order to make use of its universal and automatic jurisdiction, it is necessary that the state that the accused is a national of, without the need for a subsequent declaration, or the state that has jurisdiction where the crime occurred, be part of the Statute or accept the jurisdiction of the Court for that particular case).
- Its limited *jurisdiction* threshold for only the most serious crimes, such as:
    a) The crime of *genocide* (defined in art. 6 as a crime committed with the intention of eliminating the right to exist of national, ethnic, racial or religious communities. Said definition is supported by that which is established in the Convention for the Prevention and Sanction of the Crime of Genocide).
    b) Crimes *against humanity* (according to art. 8, understood as those crimes that for their cruelty and systematic application as part of a widespread policy, violate humanitarian principles. Such principles include bans on: slavery, torture, sex crimes, extermination, deportation or the forced movement of populations, forced disappearances of people, forced prostitution, forced pregnancy, forced sterilization [which clearly shows the hard work of NGOs in promoting the incorporation of provisions in the Statute

relating to gender], the illegal deprivation of freedom, and apartheid. In each of these cases it is necessary that the crimes are of a systematic and generalized nature, perpetrated against the civilian population as part of a state policy or committed by an organization with political ends).

c) *War crimes* (which according to art. 8 include serious violations of the Geneva Conventions from August 12, 1949, serious violations of the laws and customs of war, and, in the case of domestic conflict, serious violations of common article 3 [regarding the protection of civilians and injured or sick soldiers in battle] of the 1949 Geneva Conventions and their additional Protocol I, which explains that this will not include "situations of internal disturbances and tensions, such as riots, isolated and sporadic acts of violence and other acts of a similar nature, as not being armed conflicts." A notable part of the category of war crimes is its inclusion of the recruitment of children under the age of fifteen in the national armed forces, or of allowing the active participation of such children in the hostilities). The incorporation in this section of war crimes committed during a domestic conflict is often highlighted as one of the greatest successes of the Statute, since it is within this context, and not that of international conflicts, where the greatest levels of violence occur. As a result of this, it is all the more important to fight against impunity for accused war criminals in internal conflicts and also to prevent states from protecting such people using the excuse of having sovereignty in their own internal affairs. Despite the successes of this section, there are some who say that it is incomplete, because in the list of arms that are prohibited there is no mention of nuclear or biological weapons, or of anti-personnel mines. Also, there is nothing said about unjustified delays in the repatriation of prisoners of war, nor anything about indiscriminate attacks against the general population and civilian targets.

d) The crime of *aggression*. In theory the possibility of penalizing the crimes of terrorism[30] and drug trafficking was debated, but when no agreement about the topics could be reached, it was decided that said crimes should continue to be regulated, as they had been up until then, through treaties. Although they were also included in the debates, the categories of plane hijacking and hostage taking were also not approved for inclusion in the Statute.

- Its *complementary* character, since the creation of the International Criminal Court does not intend to substitute the obligation of every state to exercise its own criminal jurisdiction against those responsible for international crimes. Therefore, if countries follow their conventional obligations of prosecuting or extraditing those accused of violating the Conventions, the investigation and punishment of serious violations will not need to be executed by the Court. The Court will only deal with cases in which the countries involved do not carry out any investigation.
- Its *inability to apply laws retroactively*.[31] Unlike the principle of *ratione temporis*—by which facts committed in a fixed time period are judged—which was applied to the international tribunals for the Ex-Yugoslavia and Rwanda, the Rome Statute establishes the principle of prohibiting retroactively applied laws, according to which: "no person shall be criminally responsible under this Statute for conduct prior to the entry into force of the Statute." (art. 24) The criminal jurisdiction of the Court—which does not look back in time, but rather only looks towards the future—does not expire (art. 29).

30 Regarding this topic, see Matías Álvarez Dorrego, *La Corte Penal Internacional: hacia la inclusión en el Estatuto de Roma del crimen de terrorismo*, Buenos Aires, Fabián J. de Plácido, 2004.

31 Regarding the topic in general, see the recent in-depth study by José María Suárez Collía, *La retroactividad. Normas jurídicas retroactivas e irretroactivas*, Madrid, Editorial Universitaria Ramón Areces, 1rst ed., December 2005; 1rst reprint, April 2006.

- The exercise of its *jurisdiction over people and not over states,* in relation to the idea that those who commit the crimes are people and not states—the term "people" being understood as particular persons. Within this personal responsibility is included both the actual person who commits the crime and the intellectual author of the crime—like the accomplice and the person who covers up the crime, who in some way collaborate to commit the crime. In the case of genocide, the person responsible would be the direct and public instigator or whoever makes an important contribution to the execution of the crime, even though that person does not actually carry out the crime him/herself. Individual criminal responsibility cannot be excluded due to a person's official position, such as being a part of the state leadership or the government, or for forming part of a national parliament. This type of excuse would not even be valid to soften the punishment (arts. 27.1 and 27.2).
- Its *legal personality.* The Court has an international legal personality and the legal capacity necessary to fulfill its functions in the territory of any state party and, by special agreement, in the territory of any other state. With its headquarters in the Hague, it is established as a permanent institution, authorized to exercise its jurisdiction over people charged with the most serious of international crimes.

This institution is *made up of* four organs: the presidency; the appeals section (that of the first instance and that of preliminary matters); the office of the prosecutor[32] (with the ex-officio power to start an investigation regarding any viable information about a violation that the Court has jurisdiction over. This guarantees that the only cases brought before the Court will be those presented by the Security Council and countries themselves, which, due to their po-

32 Regarding this issue, see Héctor Olasolo, *Corte Penal Internacional ¿dónde investigar?: especial referencia a la Fiscalía en el proceso de activación,* preface by María del Carmen Calvo Sánchez, presentation by José Luis Rodríguez-Villasante y Prieto, introduction by Juan Antonio Yañez-Barnuevo, Valencia, Tirant Lo Blanch, 2003.

litical character, will probably select cases based on political issues more than legal ones); and the administrative department, which is linked to the United Nations.

It is necessary to point out that, although faced with the desire to include the death penalty in the Statute, which was argued for by some countries that had the death penalty within their own legal codes, the proposal did not triumph. Instead the Statute passed in Rome allows imprisonment for a maximum time period of thirty years and, in extremely serious cases, the possibility of taking into consideration a life sentence. Other punishments include fines and the confiscation of products, possessions, and assets directly or indirectly related to the crime. Another controversial proposal that in the end prevailed was to not allow trials in absentia. In addition, all sorts of legal guarantees are included, such as the principle of "*nullum crimen sine lege*," which means that nobody can be criminally responsible before the Court unless at the moment the crime was committed, said crime was clearly recognized as punishable by the Statute. At the same time, the Statute establishes that no one will be required to testify against him/herself, nor to declare him/herself guilty, thus guaranteeing the principles established in various international human rights instruments (art. 55).

2.3 Deficiencies and Limitations of the International Criminal Court: Still a Long Way to Go

Among the most recent victories in the field of human rights there has been a continued attempt to make some of the worst criminals and dictators in history personally responsible for their crimes, sending the message that leaders can no longer go on abusing their power without being punished.[33] The arrest of Pinochet, the International Criminal Tribunal for Rwanda, the trial of former Prime Minister Jean Kambada for the crime of genocide, and the case of Slobodan Milosevic all come to mind. In each and every one of

33 This is the dilemma expressed in the title of the book by Isabel Lirola Delgado – Magdalena Martín Martínez, *La Corte Penal Internacional: justicia versus impunidad*, Barcelona, Ariel, 2001.

these situations the various courts have tried to demonstrate that *nobody is above the law* and that international law imposes limits on leaders—that there is something or someone to *look after* those who are supposedly in power to protect their respective countries. This is so because in reality when crimes occur that are so grave and that are on such a grand scale, all of us are victims in some way. The international conscience would be hurt if the international community did not try to bring justice to such situations.

That is one of the reasons why the International Criminal Court had such a positive reception, which can be seen by the number of subsequent ratifications after the Rome Statute. Everyone, even the optimists, thought it would take decades for the Rome Treaty to be ratified by the necessary number of states. But it only took four years (the treaty came into force in April, 2002), and there were many other states willing to ratify the treaty in the future. As such, we can safely say that we have reached a historical milestone.[34]

As always, however, every light has its shadows, since not every country has wanted to participate. In particular there are the cases of China and Israel. Also important is the substantial rejection of the institution by the United States, the so called *master of the world*, which promoted the creation of other criminal tribunals, such as those of Yugoslavia and Rwanda, but which also did not hesitate to classify the International Criminal Court as a *monster to be eliminated*, hoping that the Court would meet a similar fate as the League of Nations.

As was already pointed out, what the U.S. really fears is that the International Criminal Court will diminish its own sovereignty and that its leaders or members of its military forces could be judged by the Court. As a result, in May 2002, the U.S. declared its opposition to the Court and did not ratify the Treaty. Still not satisfied, however, the U.S. used other methods of hurting and weakening the Court. In this vein the U.S. makes use of *impunity agreements*—bilateral agreements which, when passed, pressure other countries

34 It is classified as the last great institution of the 20th century by Ramón Ragués i Vallès, *El Tribunal Penal Internacional: la última gran institución del siglo XX*, Madrid, La Ley. Diario 2001.

not to submit U.S. nationals to the Court, with the intention of creating two systems of international law: one for the U.S. and another for the rest of the world. In addition, the U.S. Congress passed the *American Service-Member's Protection Act* (*ASPA*), which prohibits American cooperation with the Court and authorizes the president to use the appropriate means to free American personnel detained or imprisoned by the Court and to request sanctions against states that adhere to the Treaty. Keeping these objectives in mind, the United States recently cut military aid to thirty five countries that refused to sign an agreement that would impede the extradition of Americans to the International Criminal Court.[35]

2.4 International Sanctions in the World Today

To finish this section on the international criminal justice system and the International Criminal Court, I will shortly synthesize the current situation regarding international sanctions.

Currently in international law there are two distinct procedures that assure the effectiveness of international norms. On the one hand, there are *individual* actions taken directly by a state harmed by internationally unlawful actions. These measures, known as *auto-tutorage*, are characteristic of a society with a *decentralized* power structure. On the other hand, there are *collective* measures, which are measures adopted by institutions. In current international law the term "sanction" is reserved for this second type of measure, applied by virtue of the decision of an international organization. This type of measure is possible due to the rise of international *solidarity*.[36]

International organizations capable of imposing this type of sanction are those that are competent to maintain international

35 Paul Gordon Lauren, "Nuevos retos para los derechos humanos. El futuro a la luz del pasado", *op. cit.*, pp. 372-375.

36 J. Lynch, "Crime in International Perspective", in James Q. Wilson – Joan Petersilia (eds.), *Crime*, San Francisco, CA, Institute of Contemporary Studies, 1995, pp. 11-39.

peace and security—those organizations being the *United Nations* and its *regional organisms.*

In the United Nations the main competencies lie in the *Security Council* in the case of a threat to peace, deterioration of the peace or acts of aggression. This organism can make recommendations or decide the necessary measures to be taken. However, before recommendations or decisions can be made, *provisional measures* could be taken, such as the order for a cease fire, or for the withdrawal of forces in occupied territory by a set date. These measures, which come before sanctions, have as their goal the immediate and minimum establishment of a *status* of peace.

The Security Council can impose two types of *sanctions.* The first kind are sanctions that do *not* imply the use of force, which are of a *political or economic* nature, which could entail partial or total cessation of economic relations or of railroad, shipping, air, postal or telegraphic communications, and which could also include a break in diplomatic relations. There have been various situations in which the Council has applied such measures. For instance, in the case of South Africa, as a consequence of its policy of *apartheid,* in which the UN imposed an arms embargo; in the case of Rhodesia with the goal of isolating the racist regime which was established there; during the invasion of Kuwait by Iraq, etc.

On the other hand, the council can adopt sanctions that do *involve the use of force*—air, naval, or land. In situations like these, actions such as demonstrations, blockades and other similar measures would be permissible.

The insurmountable differences between the two world superpowers—the U.S. and the U.S.S.R.—during the Cold War era, along with the frequent exercise of veto power in the heart of the Security Council, led to a situation of ineffectiveness that lasted a long time.[37]

---

37 V. Gowlland-Debbas, *Collective Responses to Illegal Acts in International Law,* Dordrecht, 1990. J. Combacau, *Le pouvoir de sanctions de l'ONU (Étude théorique de la coercition militaire),* Paris, 1974. María Paz Andrés Sáenz de Santa María, "Sanciones internacionales (Derecho Inter-

The *General Assembly* of the United Nations also has jurisdiction, albeit secondary, related to imposing sanctions. The General Assembly can also make recommendations.

There are a series of issues concerning international sanctions that are useful to examine. First, such sanctions are imposed exclusively in relation to violations of international *norms* to which it is *imperative* to respond: such as acts of aggression, supporting forces of colonial domination, or serious human rights violations. The consequences of such actions mark the difference between *international offenses* and *international crimes*. In the case of the latter there exists the possibility of imposing sanctions, but for the first group there is only the simple requirement of making amends or paying reparations for the offense.

Finally, there is the issue of the *effectiveness* or actual force that the sanctions have. From a strictly legal perspective it is relevant to point out that depending on the path chosen, there is the option of making a recommendation or the option of imposing a sanction. While the first, as its name indicates, is *not* binding, the second *is*.[38]

2.5 The Survival of National Sovereignty

Sovereignty is a historical and relative concept. It is *historic* because it has a life in time, parallel to that of the existence of the state, with

nacional Público)", in *Enciclopedia Jurídica Básica*, t. IV, Madrid, Civitas, 1995, pp. 6063-6065.

38 See María José Falcón y Tella and Fernando Falcón y Tella, *Fundamento y finalidad de la sanción: ¿un derecho a castigar?*, Preface by Antonio García-Pablos, Madrid, Marcial Pons, 2005, pp. 241-243; there is an English translation by Peter Muckley, *Punishment and Culture: A Right to Punish?*, Boston-Leiden, Martinus Nijhoff Publishers, 2006. Reviewed by María Eugenia Pérez Montero, in the *Anuario de Derechos Humanos, Nueva Época*, vol. 6, Instituto de Derechos Humanos, Facultad de Derecho, Universidad Complutense de Madrid, pp. 790-798; by Ana Valero Fernández de Palencia, in *Foro. Revista de Ciencias Jurídicas y Sociales, Facultad de Derecho, Universidad Complutense de Madrid*, 2, 2005; and by José María Carabante Muntada, in *ARSP* (forhcoming).

its emergence in the 13th to 14th centuries, consolidation in the 18th century with the absolute monarchs, and its crisis, after the proclamation of the principle of the division of powers by Montesquieu. This crisis continues and is currently accentuated by the tendency to insert states into international organizations. For instance: with the creation of the European Union, the phenomenon of globalization, and the formation of an International Criminal Court. Sovereignty is *relative,* because it is the supreme level of power, the *summa postestas.* Being sovereign does not mean having *less power than* (a comparison of inferiority), having *as much power as* (a comparison of equality), or having *more power than* (a comparison of superiority), but rather having *the most power* (the supreme level).

This is made evident in the external sphere in which other states cannot interfere in the decision-making sphere of a state, which is *independent* from other states, since the other states lack jurisdiction in said country. In the domestic realm sovereignty is reflected by *superiority,* since it is the sovereign who in the end makes decisions, and it is not possible to take action against his/her resolutions.

Sovereignty took its historical form at first thanks to a single person: the *monarch* (also known as sovereign, highness, or majesty). The monarch makes reference precisely to a situation of superiority over the rest of the mortals: sovereign is the person who achieves obedience from the rest of the members of the population of one country and, nonetheless, is not required to obey anyone else. Later, sovereignty is predicated on the entire population of a state or nation. With this in mind, we can distinguish between two concepts that are not entirely equivalent: popular sovereignty and national sovereignty.

Popular sovereignty is predicated on the "people"—the population of a state—but, and this is the peculiarity, in the individual capacity of each one of its components. Thus, we say that in the exercise of popular sovereignty we exercise the right of active suffrage and we vote for our representatives in the Parliament in periodic elections. Every component of the people directly constitutes a voter and his/her vote has the same value as the vote of his/her fellow citizens: "one man, one vote."

National sovereignty is attributed to the "nation"—to the people that have a culture, folklore and language in common—but as a whole, as the collection of a specific national personality. In this way, when it ratifies an international treaty, a country strengthens itself through the exercise of its "national" sovereignty. Every component of the nation does not sign the international treaty, but rather the nation as a whole does so through its representatives.

With this brief historical and conceptual introduction in mind, we should be able to better understand the current perspective of the challenge we face today regarding the survival of sovereignty as we know it. Within this line of reasoning it is beneficial to remember, once again, the case of the U.S. in its resistance to the International Criminal Court. This resistance demonstrates just how strongly countries tend to cling to their sovereignty, even if it means going against the demands of human rights and justice. When international norms exist that put limits on national sovereignty, states cling with all their might to their jurisdictional power and try to maintain that power at any cost. The demands of human rights, however, often go down a different road: to endeavor to make *the culture of impunity become a culture of responsibility.*

Never before has sovereignty been put so much in check as is being done currently. On the one hand, every day to a greater extent, countries (especially European ones) put "self-restrictions" on their powers when those powers are legally bound to the *ratification of treaties and international declarations*—for instance those regarding human rights. On the other hand, it is also important to point out that states are now more willing to commit themselves to *humanitarian interventions.* Many such interventions, in fact, are meant to end situations of flagrant human rights violations.

Today it is clear that we are witnessing the rise of a new category of sovereignty. Unlike the sovereign monarch, national sovereignty and popular sovereignty confer the right of *individual sovereignty.* Countries are now converting into instruments of service for the people, instead of being the other way around. Individual rights are what reign supreme.

Another limit on national sovereignty comes from a realm that is greater than that of the individual. This other limit comes from the entire "global village," which considering the current boom in the phenomenon of *globalization*, goes well beyond national borders.

But not everything in this realm is a triumph. There still exist many nations that resort to their peculiarities, the specific or exceptional character of their situation, in order to continue getting around the rules of the game. In their discourse about national security they also speak of national interest. They allege that considering their circumstances a relativist approach is necessary. With this pretext in mind, said states refuse to ratify or sign human rights treaties, accept external control over their actions, or subject themselves to international jurisdiction. This will continue being a challenge in the future.[39]

3 Globalization and Human Rights

3.1 Moving towards a New World Order

With the crisis of the welfare state[40] appears a new world order. To better understand what this new world order consists of, we must begin in the postwar atmosphere, in which various political processes developed in a parallel manner.

39 See Elena Crespo Navarro, *Nuevas formas de protección del individuo en Derecho internacional. La erosión del vínculo de la nacionalidad*, Valencia, Tirant Lo Blanch, 2005, esp. pp. 379 ff. See also, Paul Gordon Lauren, "Nuevos retos para los derechos…", *cit.*, pp. 375-376.

40 Regarding this topic, see the eloquent analysis of Professor José Iturmendi Morales, Academic epilogue, "Derecho, Sanidad y derecho a la protección de la salud en un contexto social, cultural, económico y tecnológico en transformación", in the Collective Volume, compiled by Professors Eduardo Martínez y Hernández – Luis Francisco García Perulles – Enrique Barón Crespo, *Tratado del derecho a la protección de la salud*, Servicio de Publicaciones, Facultad de Derecho, Universidad Complutense de Madrid, 2004, pp. 345-687, especially epigraph V, entitled "*Crisis del Estado del Bienestar. El emergente modelo del Estado postsocial o Estado escaso. La progresiva deslegitimación de la acción política como mecanismo distribuidor de riqueza*," pp. 531-572.

First of all, two blocks of power are formed: the U.S., which develops the Marshall Plan, on the one hand, and the U.S.S.R. on the other. These were the two major powers that walked away triumphant from the great world conflict that was World War II.

Second, although there are gray areas, below these two major powers are countries like Korea, Vietnam or the countries of the Middle East. Also included in this category are countries in Western Europe that experience a resurgence—typified by the so-called "German miracle"—and that develop social democracies and free market economies, beginning a process of internalizing capital. This allows for the corresponding expansion of big American companies, especially oil companies like *Shell* and *Standard Oil*. There emerge conclaves of large European-American corporations, known as Bil meetings (named after the Hotel Bilderberg, in Holland, where the majority of these meetings took place). In a parallel fashion, in 1959 the so-called Rome Club expressed an outline for global planning in a report called "The Limits to Growth." Transnational power is the cultivating *humus* of this project of globalization.

Finally, in a large portion of the Third World begins a movement towards decolonization.

At the same time, the Church, especially after the Second Vatican Council, has a high standing with respect to the social doctrine and all that this idea refers to. Unlike the new order that others try to establish, John Paul II supported the necessity of creating appropriate organs of control and guidance that avoid human rights violations. At the same time, these organs would value personal dignity and equality amongst all peoples, viewing the "other" in a supportive fashion—not as an enemy or as an instrument, but rather as fellow man. In this way a field of action and struggle is opened in the name of social justice, and many NGO's and international organizations make the goal of social justice their motto and purpose.

This postmodern and post-industrial society is a global civilization. The axis of this society is information and knowledge: this is what economists call the passage from an "*economy of goods and services*" to an "*economy of information*." The group that experiences the fastest social rise in this society is the group of technicians, professionals and administrators linked to this new type of intellectual technology. The key concept is efficiency. The "*middle classes*" that want to climb the social ladder are the driving force of change, as opposed to the rich and prosperous classes. The basis of this system is refinement and "*cutting-edge technology*."

Faced with transnational power and the project of globalization,[41] the world introduced at a strange and dangerous time for man, with a threatening nature that was never before known, the beginning of a growing situation of uprooting in which one can see the paradox that the human being is at the same time *the most caring and the most lonely creature*. In this new political logic, patriotism is considered a tribal feeling and the state is considered the political community—something artificial and unstable. Along with this global project comes an economic expression (that of the transnational) and a social expression (that of the consumer). With the great boom experienced by technology,[42] says Jürgen Habermas, the technocratic conscience assumes the role of an ideology that replaces bourgeois ideologies.

Notions of identity and national sovereignty are put into question, as is the very concept of politics as a public movement, and due to this setback the private realm emerges as a priority. The belief is that the common good will be achieved by allowing everyone to freely pursue their specific goals. The paradox then comes to light that the latest technology can lead to discoveries that prolong life and at the same time provoke, amongst other scars on society,

---

41 See Juan Antonio Carrillo Salcedo, *Globalización y orden internacional: lección inaugural leída en la solemne apertura del Curso Académico 2004-2005 en la Universidad de Sevilla,* Sevilla, Universidad, 2004. Carles Casals, *Globalización: apuntes de un proceso que está transformando nuestras vidas*, Barcelona, Interpón, 2001.

42 Regarding globalization and new technologies see, among others, Víctor Manuel Marí Sáez, *Globalización, nuevas tecnologías y comunicación*, Madrid, Ediciones de la Torre, 1999. Rosa Isabel Montes Mendoza (comp.), *Globalización y nuevas tecnologías: nuevos retos y ¿nuevas reflexiones?,* Madrid, Organización de Estados Iberoamericanos para la Educación, la Ciencia y la Cultura, 2001. María Laura Pardo – María Valentina Noelia (eds.); Laura Aranovich (*et al.*), *Globalización y nuevas tecnologías*, Buenos Aires, Biblos, 2000.

terrorism, wars and holocausts. Ludwig von Mises claims that man chooses the means to different ends, leaving behind in this choice important ethical principles and notions of values.[43]

The bipolar world (of the U.S. and U.S.S.R.) has collapsed and what has emerged is a multi-polar one. Despite the fall of the Berlin Wall, many styles of former totalitarian and authoritarian governments have not been totally defeated, and there still exists the risk that they will gain new strength. Different forms of religious fundamentalism have shown up. International terrorism gains a new dimension after events like those of September 11, 2001 in New York and Washington or those of March 11, 2004 in Madrid.[44] These acts provoke preventive wars or wars of anticipation, as opposed to defensive wars which have traditionally been considered the only type of legitimate warfare.

3.2 General Considerations Regarding Globalization

We find ourselves on the path towards a new worldwide international law, a new stage in humanity.[45] There has been an evolu-

43 María Cristina Campagna - Alfredo Mason, *Teoría del Estado. Cuando la filosofía y la política construyen la realidad*, Buenos Aires, Editorial Biblos, 1997, pp. 201-215.

44 Vid. regarding the same topic, Michael Mann (et al.), *La globalización y el 11 de septiembre*, Madrid, Akal, 2001.

45 Regarding the topic, José Iturmendi Morales, "¿Hacia un nuevo Derecho Internacional?", in the *Anuario de Derechos Humanos, Nueva Época, vol.* 2, Instituto de Derechos Humanos, Facultad de Derecho. Universidad Complutense de Madrid, Madrid, 2001, pp. 523-779, esp. p. 777: "*Perhaps it would be preferable to remember the Habermasean proposal in favor of a transformation in the cosmopolitan sense of the state of nature between the nation states into an authentic legal order in which they should not necessarily (and going against what was affirmed by Georges Renard—1876-1943) give considerations of security priority over considerations of justice. It was well put by the master Legaz y Lacambra: 'in the international order, as in any sector of the legal order, justice can only be achieved with order and security; but justice is the only condition which assures a lasting security and order.'* " With a similar title to the previous work, but replacing the word "internacional" for the term "mundial," in

tion from the concept of traditional "*parishioners*" (of those that only worry about their surroundings), to the concept of "*subjects*" (those that pay attention to the laws, for example the right to vote), and finally to the modern concept of "*citizens*" of the global village (among which there already exists a civic culture).[46]

The Machiavellian concept of the state, as that which "is" and that which endures (in relation to the word "establishment"), is something which remains in time and outlives the people who created it. The school of neo-liberal thought in certain American universities (e.g. Stanford, Harvard, Yale, etc.) has come to coin a term that currently provokes furor and is clearly in style: *globalization*.[47] Today we talk about the world not as a plurality of fragmented states, but rather as a "global village," strongly linked at all levels: economic,[48]

exact relation to the phenomenon of globalization, Hermann Tertsch, "¿Hacia un nuevo orden mundial?", in Pablo Badillo O'Farrell (coord.), *Pluralismo, tolerancia, multiculturalismo..., op. cit.*, pp. 233-245.

46 Regarding this topic see, Enrique Martín López, *La sociedad global*, Madrid, Fundación para la Formación de Altos Profesionales, 1997. Elena Crespo Navarro, *Nuevas formas de protección del individuo en Derecho internacional. La erosión del vínculo de la nacionalidad*, Valencia, Tirant Lo Blanch, 2005.

47 An article about the topic that has been printed in and welcomed by various international magazines is "Globalización y Derecho Internacional" by Professor Pedro de Vega García, that was published in the volume 100 of *Revista de Estudios Políticos*. Also regarding the topic, see Mariano Aguirre – Teresa Filesi – Mabel González, *Globalización y sistema internacional: Anuario CIP 2000*, Barcelona, Icaria (etc.), 2000. José Antonio Álvarez Merayo – Maximiliano Fernández Fernández – Pilar Bena Bua (coords.), *La globalización y sus efectos en los inicios del tercer milenio: actas del ciclo organizado por la Universidad Católica de Ávila, Ávila, 15 de febrero a 5 de abril de 2001*, Ávila, Universidad Católica de Ávila, 2001. Pia Locatelli "Globalización, un proceso en marcha," in Dolors Renau (coord.), Micaela Navarro (et al.), *Globalización y mujer*, Madrid, Pablo Iglesias, 2002. Alfonso López – Pepe Gálvez, *La globalización: pasen y vean*, Barcelona, Icaria, 2002.

48 Regarding economic globalization, see, among others, Jacques Adda, *La globalización de la economía: orígenes y desafíos*, Spanish translation by Javier Ortega, in collaboration with Fernando Minguez and the final revision by the author, Madrid, Sequitur, 1999. Ramón Alós – Pere Jódar, "Glo-

balización económica, cambios en los modelos de empresa, segmentación del trabajo y relaciones laborales," in Ramón Alós (*et al.*), *Sindicalismo y globalización*, Madrid, Confederación Sindical de Comisiones Obreras, 2002. Margarita Barañana Cid, *La globalización económica: incidencia en las relaciones sociales y económicas*, Madrid, Consejo General del Poder Judicial, 2002. Maite Barea – Margarita Billón, *Globalización y nueva economía*, Madrid, Encuentro, 2002. Alessandro Bonanno (coord.), *Globalización del sector agrícola y alimentario*, Madrid, Ministerio de Agricultura, Pesca y Alimentación, 1994. Michael D. Bordo – Antu Panini Murshid, *Globalization and Changing Patterns in the International Transmission of Shocks in Financial Markets*, Cambridge – Massachusetts –, National Bureau of Economic Research, 2002. *La globalización en beneficio de todos: la Unión Europea y el comercio mundial*, Luxemburgo, Oficina de Publicaciones Oficiales de las Comunidades Europeas, 2003. Congreso IREC 2001, *Conferencia sobre relaciones laborales en Europa (2001, Madrid), Globalización, competitividad y gobierno del empleo y de las condiciones de empleo en Europa: estructuras, actores y estrategias: estado de la cuestión. Organizada por la Escuela de Relaciones Laborales de la Universidad Complutense de Madrid, con la colaboración de la Facultad de Ciencias Políticas y Sociología de la UCM*, Madrid, s. n., 2001. Congreso Regional Americano de Derecho del Trabajo y de la Seguridad Social (4. 1998. Santiago de Chile), *Globalización económica y derecho individual del trabajo*, Santiago de Chile, Sociedad Internacional de Derecho del Trabajo y de la Seguridad Social, 1998. Jaime Estay – Alicia Girón – Osvaldo Martínez (comp.), *La globalización de la economía mundial: principales dimensiones en el umbral del siglo XXI*, México, Universidad Nacional Autónoma de México, Instituto de Investigaciones Económicas, 1999. Santiago García Echevarría, *Globalización de la economía y dinámica de cambio de la empresa comercial: hacia una nueva cultura empresarial*, Alcalá de Henares, Universidad de Alcalá, Instituto de Dirección y Organización de Empresa, 1995. Beatriz Herrera García, *Globalización y sistema financiero*, Lima, Fondo Editorial Universidad Nacional Mayor de San Marcos, 2003. Juan E. Iranzo Martín, *Globalización y nueva economía*, Madrid, Instituto de Estudios Económicos, 2003. Paul R. Krugman, *La globalización de la economía y las crisis financieras: lecciones de economía*, La Coruña, Instituto de Estudios Económicos de Galicia Pedro Barrié de la Maza, 1999. Hans J. Michelmann, (*et al.*), *Globalization and Agricultural Trade Policy*, Boulder Co., Lynne Rienner Publishers, 2001. Mercedes Molina Ibañez, *La globalización económica a debate*, Madrid, Instituto Complutense de Estudios Internacionales, 1998. Maurice Obstfeld – Alan M. Taylor, *Globalization and Capital Markets*, Cambridge – Massachusetts –, National

educational,[49] and on a communicative or linguistic level (with English currently serving as the clearly established global language). The subject of globalization has a great impact on human rights issues.[50] In this area we have witnessed the importance of the decisive push that new information and communication technologies, especially the Internet, have given to the phenomenon of globalization. To the extent that today every cybernaut can communicate without spatial limitations, with the actual speaker in real time, the "global village" has become a "global home," a "global *living-room*" or a "global studio."[51]

We should perhaps also lament the fact that the globalization of necessities has been forgotten. This type of globalization, as its necessary consequence, should have accompanied the globalization of resources.[52] The globalization of cultures has also been forgot-

---

Bureau of Economic Research, 2002. Iliana Olivié Aldasoro, *Globalización financiera y crisis en economías emergentes: análisis teórico y estudio de los casos de México (1994) y Corea del Sur (1997)*, Thesis, Universidad Complutense de Madrid, Facultad de Ciencias Económicas y Empresariales, Departamento de Economía Aplicada I, directed by Pablo Bustelo Gómez, 2002. Madrid, Servicio de Publicaciones de la Universidad Complutense de Madrid, 2004. Enrique Palazuelos Manso, *La globalización financiera: la internalización del capital financiero a finales del siglo XX*, Madrid, Síntesis, 1998.

49 Regarding globalization and education, we would like to highlight the work of Mariano Aguirre (*et al.*), José Ignacio Flor (coord.), *Globalización, crisis ambiental y educación*, Madrid, Ministerio de Educación, Cultura y Deporte, Secretaría General Técnica, 2002. *Globalización y educación*, Pamplona, Universidad de Navarra, 2001.

50 As some studies reflect, such as those by María José Fariñas Dulce, *Globalización, ciudadanía y derechos humanos*, "Cuadernos Bartolomé de las Casas," 16, Madrid, Dykinson, 2000. Asier Martínez de Bringas, *Globalización y derechos humanos*, Bilbao, Universidad de Deusto, 2001.

51 Antonio-Enrique Pérez Luño, *La tercera generación de derechos humanos*, Navarra, Thomson-Aranzadi, 2006, pp. 245-246.

52 *Vid.* regarding the topic, with a critical view, Zygmunt Bauman, *La globalización: consecuencias humanas*, translation by Daniel Zadunaisky, México (etc.), Fondo de Cultura Económica, 1999. 2nd ed. in Spanish, 2001; 2nd ed. in Spanish, 1rst reprint. 2003. Joan Bestard Comas, *Glo-*

balización, tercer mundo y solidaridad: estudio comparativo entre los Informes del Programa de las Naciones Unidas para el Desarrollo (PNUD) y los documentos de la Doctrina Social de la Iglesia (DSI), Madrid, Biblioteca de Autores Cristianos, 2003. Michel Chossudovsky, *Globalización de la pobreza y nuevo orden mundial,* 1st ed. in Spanish, Buenos Aires, Siglo Veintiuno, 2002. Guillermo de la Dehesa, *Globalización, desigualdad y pobreza,* Madrid, Alianza, 2003. Richard Falk, *La globalización depredadora: una crítica,* Spanish translation by Herminia Bevia and Antonio Resines, Madrid, Siglo Veintiuno de España, 2002. Mariona Farré – Rafael Allepuz (eds.), *Globalización y dependencia: efectos de la mundialización sobre el desarrollo de los pueblos,* Lleida, Edicions de la Universitat de Lleida, 2001.Ramón Fernández Durán – Miren Etxezarreta – Manolo Sáez Bayona, *Globalización capitalista: luchas y resistencias,* Barcelona, Virus, 2001. Foro "Ignacio Ellacuría" Solidaridad y Cristianismo, *Conferencias sobre la globalización y sus excluidos,* Estella (Navarra), Verbo Divino, 1999. 3rd ed., 2002. Susan George (*et al.*), edition by Matthew J. Gibney, *La globalización de los derechos humanos,* Spanish translation from *Globalizing Rights,* Barcelona, Crítica, 2004. *Globalización, crecimiento y pobreza: construyendo una economía mundial incluyente,* Washington, Banco Mundial; Bogotá, Alfaomega, Cop. 2002. Alfredo Guerra-Borges, *Globalización e integración latinoamericana,* México, Siglo XXI, 2002. Bernard Gillochon, *La globalización: ¿un futuro para todos?,* Barcelona, Spes, 2003. David Held (1951-) – Anthony McGrew, *Globalización – Antiglobalización: sobre la reconstrucción del orden mundial,* Spanish translation by Andrés De Francisco, Barcelona (etc.), Paidós, 2003. José C. Lisón Arcal, *La globalización que nos quieren vender,* Madrid, Nivela, 2003. Josep F. Mària i Serrano, *La globalización,* Barcelona, Christianisme i Justicia, D. L., 2000. María Maesso Corral – Raquel González Blanco (coords.), *La globalización, oportunidades y desafíos,* Cáceres, Universidad de Extremadura, Servicio de Publicaciones, 2003. Victoriano Martín, "Globalización, reo o fiscal," in Paloma de Villota (ed.), *Globalización a qué precio: el impacto en las mujeres del norte y del sur,* Barcelona, Icaria Antrazyt, 2001. Jorge Francisco Malem Seña, *Globalización, comercio internacional y corrupción,* Barcelona, Gedisa, 2000. José Peláez Marón (coord.), *Globalización, deuda externa y exigencias de justicia social,* Tres Cantos (Madrid), Akal, 2003. Diego Pereyra, *Globalización, hegemonía y crisis: una mirada crítica sobre la globalidad y las transformaciones del capitalismo mundial,* Buenos Aires, Eudeba, 1999. Juan José Sánchez Inarejos, *La globalización al desnudo: un viaje desde la realidad económica y tecnológica hasta lo más íntimo del corazón humano,* Madrid, Chaos-Entropy, D. L., 2001. Jan

ten.[53] In fact, globalization and multiculturalism could not be more different in their origins. Multiculturalism, of course, is another one of the phenomena and expressions currently in style.

But, what exactly is culture?[54] The term culture is perhaps abused nowadays, with the understanding that every peculiarity and uniqueness, for the mere fact of being a distinguishing characteristic, can be considered culture. In reality when we talk about the existence of culture in the strict sense of the term, what is meant is not just an ethnicity and folklore, a common language and shared traditions, but also, in line with the phenomenon of the three-dimensional, an identity based around values and norms.[55]

Another one of the failures of globalization, in contrast to its obvious successes which are well known, is related to multiculturalism. Said failure is the migratory ebb tide that globalization has given rise to. If historically one could speak of an "invasion of savages," which is how peoples that lived beyond the borders of what constituted the civilized world were viewed, today we are witnessing an authentic invasion in the form of immigration to countries of the Western world. This migratory movement has developed in

---

Aart Scholte, *Globalization: a Critical Introduction*, London, MacMillan Press, 2000. John Saxe-Fernández (coord.), *Globalización: crítica a un paradigma*, México, Universidad Nacional Autónoma de México, Plaza & Janés, 1999. John Saxe-Fernández – James Petras – Henry Veltmeyer – Omar Nuñez, *Globalización, imperialismo y clase social*, Buenos Aires-México, Úmen, 2001. Juan José Toribio, *Globalización, desarrollo y pobreza*, Madrid, Círculo de Empresarios, 2003.

53 See Joaquín Brünner, *Globalización cultural y posmodernidad*, Santiago de Chile (etc.), Fondo de Cultura Económica, 1st ed., 2nd reprint, 2002.

54 Regarding the subject of culture in relation to globalization, see John Tomlinson, *Globalización y cultura*, Spanish translation by Fernando Martínez Valdés, technical revision by José Luis González Martínez, México, Oxford University Press, 2001. George Yúdice, *Globalización de la cultura y nueva sociedad*, Caracas, Cipost, 1997.

55 Regarding globalization and culture, see the study of Dolors Comas D'Argemir, "La globalización, ¿unidad del sistema?: exclusión social, diversidad y diferencia cultural en la aldea global", in Noam Chomsky (*et al.*), *Los límites de la globalización*, Barcelona, Ariel, 2002.

the most underprivileged cultures and nations of the world, and is a phenomenon that poses many social and legal problems.[56]

The issue of immigration is clearly connected to the subject of pluralism and tolerance, as values proclaimed by our cultures. It is also linked to the issue of respect for minorities and the principle of majority rule, which dominates current democratic systems. Finally, the immigration problem is also related to the subject of individual autonomy.[57]

3.3 The Differences between the Concepts of Worldization, Globalization and Universalization

It is necessary at this point to clarify what is meant by terms that are not exactly the same, although there is only a thin line that separates them. These terms are "worldization," "globalization" and "universalization."[58] At the *Facultés Universitaires Saint-Louis* in Brussels, Professor François Ost specifies and distinguishes between:

---

56 This is the subject of the work *Globalización, migraciones y desarrollo: Informe del Milenio, Propuestas Claves para el Milenio, Declaración del Milenio*, Madrid, Movimiento Contra la Intolerancia, 2001? Regarding the same topic, also see Sandro Mezzadra, *Derecho de fuga. Migraciones, ciudadanía y globalización*, translation by Miguel Santucho, Madrid, 2005.

57 Related to the subject, Juan Antonio Martínez Muñoz, "Multiculturalismo y estados personales," in the *Anuario de Derechos Humanos, Nueva Época*, volumen 2, Instituto de Derechos Humanos, Facultad de Derecho, Universidad Complutense de Madrid, Madrid, 2001, pp. 779-837, esp. pp. 779-790. In this article the solution that is proposed against the notion of territorial states is the creation of—as the title makes evident—personal states (estados personales).

58 François Ost, "Mundialización, globalización y universalización: abandonar, ahora y siempre, el estado de naturaleza", in *Anuario de Derechos Humanos, Nueva Época*, vol. 3, Instituto de Derechos Humanos, Facultad de Derecho, Universidad Complutense, Madrid, 2002, pp. 453-493, esp. p. 465: "*The question that we ask ourselves today is whether we know if worldization, or more precisely the worldizations (economic interdependences, migratory flows, integration of communication networks, cultural hybridizations,...), changing the spatial scale of problems, are not in fact*

1 "*Worldization*" today is an uncontestable fact which results in the intensification of global interdependencies in multiple areas of social life, which goes beyond the classic concept of a border, and which causes the distinction between interior/exterior to lose force. We can see this is the case considering that military policies are defined by huge supranational alliances (NATO), and that economic policies are determined in global (WTO, IMF) or regional meeting grounds. Within the European Union, states have even lost some of their traditional privileges.

2 "*Globalization*," although generally considered nothing more than a translation of the term "mondialisation," for the Belgian author presents an *ideological* meaning, in strictly economic terms, that favors effectiveness and competition, and has a tendency towards the commercialization of all aspects of social life and its legal liberalization. Globalization has as its only dominant and unilateral thought: "*all that is the market is real, all that is real is the market.*"

3 "*Universalization*," which is also an ideological concept, is the aspiration to reinterpret the fact of worldization by endowing it with meaning through, for instance, the role of human rights as a universal vocation.

---

creating imbalances between these problems and the regulatory capacity of states. Is the state still in the condition to guarantee the security of its residents, considering that now it has to share sovereignty over its territory with other powers in advance? Is the state still the place to build social bonds, considering that identities are now of a plural nature and given that multiple citizens cross over its territory?...Finally, can the state still insure the consistency of the safety-net of social security, a guarantee against exclusion, considering that the state has lost a good part of its mastery in the management of the main levers of the national economy?" See Fernando Falcón y Tella, "Valeurs, Norms et Faits dans le Droit", in *Revue Interdisciplinaire d'Études Juridiques*, 53, December 2004, pp. 123-139.

Worldization would be considered more on the level of verifiable facts, *globalization* on the level of economic rules, and *universalization* perhaps more in an axiological/values-based world.[59]

Aside from François Ost, there are other authors that make the distinction between globalization and worldization by considering the first the *cause* and the second the *effect* of the dominance of capitalism. Either way, the issue involves concepts that are both complex and ambiguous, and that vary according to who makes use of them. There is no shortage of people who speak of worldization as a growing interdependence of the *territories* and nations of the planet, and speak of globalization as the *current phase* in this historical process of interdependence—a phase characterized by inequality. In short, some theorists simply consider the first term as the *Anglo-Saxon* designation and the second as the *French-speaking* way of expressing the same idea.

3.4 Some Pending Subjects about Globalization

It seems clear that globalization is the unification of the global society according to capitalist principles—the commercialization of the world—at all levels: economic and financial, communicative, cultural, ideological or political. But globalization is not a synonym for the internalization of values, human rights, democracy or certain freedoms. Neo-liberal globalization frequently violates fundamental human rights—just as much so economic, social and cultural rights as civil and political rights. The forces that control globalization are more interested in economic benefits than in the well-being of the most underprivileged nations. For instance, in Africa there is a serious problem with AIDS, to the point that more than thirty

59 What will be the future of globalization? Attempting to answer this question, see Concepción Ortega – María José Guerra (comp.); María Xosé Agra (*et al.*), *Globalización y neoliberalismo: ¿un futuro inevitable?*, Oviedo, Nobel, 2002. Eugenio Ortega Riquelme, *La globalización en la encrucijada: sociedad, política y mercado en un mundo globalizado*, Buenos Aires, Lom, 2002.

million Africans carry the disease.[60] Nonetheless, the large pharmaceutical industries refuse to facilitate access to anti-retroviral drugs (ARV) for the sick. What's more, cultural imperialism which comes from a model of civilization based on Western values—which are the values that lay the foundation for globalization—is causing the disappearance of age-old cultures and diverse native languages in favor of the dominance of English, which has clearly become the language of the global economy. It is in these circumstances in which there has also originated a process of "resistance" against the loss of the unique characteristics of various peoples, giving rise to a phenomenon which conflicts with globalization. This movement consists of the fragmentation of national identities, which Andrew Mair has called the phenomenon of "glocalization" and James Rosenau that of "fragmegration." Regarding the subject of the environment, there is condemnation for a process of desertification and deforestation of a large part of the planet. This process influences climactic changes, producing natural disasters such as hurricanes and cyclones. In addition, oceans are being contaminated and fragile coastal ecosystems are being destroyed. The phenomenon of globalization has been helped by a revolution in computer technology and by a similar revolution in telecommunications. It is the final stage in a process that began with the discovery of the New World. Globalization, in its neo-liberal sense, began in the mid-19th century, but its most recent phase began just three decades ago. In this new process of globalization we are witnessing the replacement of the *civilizing mission* of the colonial era by *liberal proselytism*.[61]

60 Mbuyi Kabunda, "Globalización y derechos humanos en África," in Various Authors., *La globalización y los derechos humanos, IV Jornadas Internacionales de Derechos Humanos* (Sevilla, 2003), Talasa Ediciones, pp. 60-90.

61 Regarding the first aspect, that of the "civilizing mission" of the colonial age, see Martti Koskenniemi, *El discreto civilizador de naciones. El auge y caída del Derecho internacional 1870-1960*, Spanish translation by Natalia Zaragozá García, revised by Paula Alberro and Fernando Falcón y Tella, from the 1st edition in English -*The Gentle Civilizer of Nations. The Rise and Fall of International Law 1870-1960*, Cambridge, Cambridge University Press, 2001-, published in Buenos Aires-Madrid, Ciudad Ar-

3.5 *Globalization and Immigration*

For the forces of globalization to be coherent in their ideology of the free market, they must also permit a free market of ideas and the free circulation of people, in the same way that they foster the free circulation of capital and goods on a global scale. Nevertheless, the free circulation of people currently has its limits, due to the obstacles that countries put in place in order to keep problematic migratory phenomena under control. Is it acceptable that our modern democratic, globalized society of the 21st century limits such a right, that of *jus migrandi et illic degendi*, which was historically recognized as *jus humanitatis*—a part of the universal patrimony of humanity? It was Francisco de Vitoria, in his *Relectio de Indis*, who made the first legal construction of *jus migrandi* by pointing out:

> *In all nations it is considered inhuman to poorly treat and poorly receive transients without having a just cause for doing so. Just the opposite should occur—foreigners should be treated well, with humanity and courtesy.*

This author also shows the possible limits of this *jus migrandi et illic degendi*, which consist of the peaceful establishment of the immigrants as well as efforts by the immigrants not to provoke the impoverishment of the native population. It is in the 20th century when more important limits to people's freedom of movement are introduced, paradoxically when we find ourselves in a globalized world that supports the free market and a society of information—especially due to the Internet. With the consolidation of national states there emerged the concept of borders and the distinction between nationals and foreigners. Only the extension of the system of human rights—especially in its most recent generations—as a universal system would be capable of encouraging a resolution of said dichotomy. With the extension of this system we would also avoid precariousness and discrimination—problems that currently affect the rights and liberties of foreigners. Precariousness is a problem

gentina-Servicio de Publicaciones de la Facultad de Derecho de la Universidad Complutense de Madrid, 2005.

since foreigners are often either not allowed to enter a country or are expelled from a country that they entered in the past. Discrimination is a problem because immigrants do not enjoy their rights in conditions of equality. This goes against the principle of equality, which is one of the basic pillars of the rule of law.

Keeping these ideas in mind, article 13 of the *Universal Declaration of Human Rights* says:

1. *Everyone has the right to freedom of movement and residence within the borders of each state.*
2. *Everyone has the right to leave any country, including his own, and to return to his country.*

The literal meaning of said precept is ambiguous and vague, which has led to conflicting interpretations. For some, the article only recognizes the freedom of movement and residence within the territory of one state. For others the freedom of movement as it is recognized in the Declaration is not restricted to the interior of one state, considering the terms used are "each state" and not "his/her state" or the "state of his/her nationality." The *jus peregrinandi*, or right to leave, would be meaningless if it did not rely on a correlative right to enter. It would be difficult to exercise the right to leave if one could not at the same time enter another territory.

This is not to say that internal legislation does not later regulate this right. There is a practical necessity to do so. But from a strictly theoretical perspective, if said right stops being universal so it can have exclusions—for instance regarding foreigners who are not administratively documented—then it is no longer a fundamental human right, since it is no longer something that is inseparable from a human person.

On the other hand, the *jus migrandi et illic degendi* includes the "right to emigrate and to establish yourself in a different country other than your own," but also includes the "right not to emigrate." There must be freedom at the moment of making the choice, because if there is not, then it is not a right we are witnessing but rather an "obligation." Economic globalization, by being a source of inequalities between the populations of poor and rich countries, diminishes this freedom of choice and forces the current massive migrations we are experiencing. This involves the uprooting of peoples as well as important social costs—familial and personal sacrifices for those that emigrate. There are also important legal and social problems for the host countries that the emigrants flock to. In this situation the notion that the establishment of the immigrants be peaceful and not provoke the impoverishment of either the natives or the immigrants emerges as a necessary condition for the legitimate exercise of *jus migrandi*. All rights have their limits. Mutual respect is necessary—the observance of the rights of others by both sides. Simply put, not everything goes. Health and public security function as possible limits to the right of emigration. Both the receiving population and the emigrant population should be economically, socially, personally and culturally enriched.[62]

When we talk about migration and globalization—the latter as a phenomenon that leads to exceeding *limits* and leads to displacement in relation to *globalization from below*—it is necessary to point out the existence of a large division between the *jus sanguinis* model, that shapes the citizen community in a restrictive way as a community of descendents, and the *jus soli* model, that defines the citizen community in expansive theoretical terms as a territorial community. It is no coincidence then that inflexibility towards immigrants, which characterized the 1990s in Europe, has been accompanied by growing pressures to introduce elements of *jus sanguinis*. In many countries of the European Union there has been a tendency in recent years to guarantee the social, economic and political rights of immigrants regardless of whether or not they have formally been admitted to the citizenship of that country. The status of legal personality—based on the universal character of human rights recognized and guaranteed by the United Nations and by international treaties—has tended to replace the status of citizenship as the origin of immigrant rights. In these circumstances it is useful to reference the English term *denizenship*, coined in the

62 Pascual Aguelo Navarro, "Derechos y libertades de los extranjeros," in *La globalización y los derechos humanos. IV Jornadas Internacionales de Derechos Humanos (Sevilla, 2003)*, Talasa Ediciones, pp. 90-102.

16th century to designate the position of the foreigner that was accepted as a citizen thanks to a concession by the crown. This same term can be used to indicate the condition of those immigrants that, although they did not previously acquire the new citizenship of a certain country, benefit from a series of rights that belong to citizens, due to these immigrants' legal and permanent residence in that country. These immigrants receive a sort of second-class citizenship, *authorized —octroyé—* through the aforementioned permission of residence, that for immigrants is equivalent to the Arendtian *right to have rights.*[63]

3.6 The Impact of Globalization on Law

The phenomenon of globalization falls into a field of special relevance on the level of state jurisdiction: on the level of the sources of law. At this point nowadays the main characteristic is the *normative supra-nationality*, that manifests itself through the incorporation of states into international or supranational organizations, which allows them to have common legal rules in place. As a result there has been an attempt to create a new *jus commune*, or a universal law, that in a similar fashion as the universal law forged by medieval universities, will surpass national borders. One of the challenges of our time, in accordance with the title of this section—"the impact of globalization on law"—is the university education of jurists worldwide. This education surpasses the traditional split between continental systems (those of *civil law*) and Anglo Saxon systems (those of *common law*).

This tendency towards universalization can be clearly seen in the field of human rights. Actually, today we speak of the value of the universality of human rights, which had been limited over a long period of time by the exercise of state sovereignty. Currently, however, with growing intensity states are curtailing their sovereignty by ratifying international instruments and declarations that are devot-

63 Sandro Mezzadra, *Derecho de fuga. Migraciones, ciudadanía y globalización*, Spanish translation by Miguel Santucho, Madrid, Traficantes de Sueños, 2005, esp. pp. 47-49 and 98-108.

ed to human rights. What happens is that, since the phenomenon of globalization has a clear neo-liberal/capitalistic influence, from the point of view of philosophy and legal theory and human rights, this influence is expressed in the *boom in and globalization of guarantees of individual rights*—first generation rights—and a resulting *weakening of economic, social and cultural rights—second generation rights.* The concentration of profit in First World countries (the global wealthy) and the correlative impoverishment of Third World countries (the global poor) point out how Eurocentrism and neo-imperialism are enemies of globalization. Global habits of consumption are created that standardize fashion trends and/or ways of life. This phenomenon has become known as the *"McDonaldization of the world."* As a result we have seen emphasized the asymmetry and inequality apparent in the enjoyment of freedom.

It should be pointed out here that globalization *is not a value.* It is a *descriptive* concept, unlike the concepts of universalism and cosmopolitism, with which globalization is often confused since it promotes the other two ideas. What is certain is that globalization is a concept that describes particular characteristics relating to the functioning of economic, social, political, cultural and legal processes in the world today.[64]

4 The Most Recent Generations of Human Rights

4.1 First and Second Generation Rights. Conceptual Difference

When discussing the topic of human rights, it is common to refer to the existence of a series of generations. Authors speak of a first and second generation of rights, of a third, and at least according to some, also a fourth. It is an attempt to theoretically cover all the different categories of existing rights. As with all theoretical constructions, that of the different generations of rights has its dangers, its bright spots, and also its shadows. Among the possible risks that

64 Antonio-Enrique Pérez Luño, *La tercera generación de derechos humanos, op. cit.*, pp. 243-254.

this construction could entail, there is one that a large number of theories have in common. This risk is the assumption of a confinement, inflexibility, and a lack of elasticity when categorizing rights, which goes against the richness and changing multiplicities of life. This approach pigeonholes rights into rigid clichés, as if one were dealing with watertight compartments, when in reality rights are interrelated and introduce fluid and fluctuating borders. Thus there are hybrid rights, such as the right to education, which is situated between the first and second generations, and others, like the right to a healthy environment, which is located between the second and third generations.

Another risk of this theoretical distinction is that of converting the chronological priority into an axiological priority, changing—the redundancy is helpful here—first generation rights not only into the first ones in time, but rather also into the most important ones, considering that there are first, second, and third quality rights.

It is also helpful to think about how the generational theory of rights leads to the inevitable attainment of these generations, which appear to be produced in an inevitable fashion, when in reality there are risks of backward movement and the future does not always bring about progress. Certainly, law is a constant fight: the fight for rights.[65]

Often mentioned as first and second generation rights are those included in the Spanish Constitution under the heading of "derechos fundamentales y libertades públicas" (fundamental rights and public freedoms)—Chapter II of Title I, articles 15-29—and the "principios rectores de la política social y económica" (the governing principles of social and economic policy)—Chapter III of Title I, articles 39-52—respectively. Examples of first generation rights are the right to life or the right to privacy (included as civil rights) or the active and passive right to vote (amongst political rights).

65 Aniza Fernanda García Morales, *La justiciabilidad de los derechos económicos, sociales y culturales (desc)*, Tesina de Especialista en Derechos Humanos, Instituto de Derechos Humanos, Madrid, Servicio de Publicaciones, Facultad de Derecho, Universidad Complutense de Madrid, 2003, pp. 25-26.

Examples of second generation rights are the right to property or the right to social security benefits (amongst economic rights), the right to worthy housing (amongst social rights), or all the rights relating to scientific production (such as cultural rights).

First and second generation rights, as the name itself indicates, were those that obtained an earlier recognition in international texts. Thus, civil and political rights already appear in legal declarations of a liberal nature from the 18th century—the French Declaration of the Rights of Man and of the Citizen in 1789 and the Bill of Rights of the "good people of Virginia," in the U.S. in 1776. Economic, social and cultural rights find recognition in the international covenant of 1966 that bears that name.

Perhaps it would make sense to ask why we allude to such rights in a book such as the one the reader has in his/her hands that bears the title "Challenges for human rights," if these rights have been consolidated and recognized since the 18th century. The answer is clear if we keep certain facts in mind. For instance, the USA PATRIOT ACT, put into law by the great world power that is the United States with the stated purpose of protecting against a lack of security and future risks that the current threat of international terrorism implies since the attacks of 9/11, as do other previous and subsequent terrorist attacks—such as those that took place in Moscow, Bali, Kikambala, Riyadh, Istanbul, Madrid, or London. This law does real harm to some rights, especially those of the first generation, such as the right to privacy or the right to the secrecy and confidentiality of communications. As such, the saying of the deceased professor of criminal law and judge, Marino Barbero Santos, with which he closes an article referring to the death penalty, is a relevant one, and in effect says: "*one should not stop watching over their weapons.*"

As a result, once again we must affirm that there is still a long path ahead of us, and with regards to what we are discussing here, it would be suitable at least *not to start taking steps backwards* over the parts of the path we have already crossed. This is the reason why, by way of a succinct synthesis, I will point out some of the distinctive features between first and second generation rights that make up, or at least should make up, the *hard center*, the very core of national and international legislation and policy.

Very briefly one could affirm that first generation rights are *absolute and binding, subject to judicial review* (whose required fulfillment can be demanded in a coercively direct manner), and are rights that generate in the state a simple obligation of *abstention*—what is known as an *obligation of results*. This obligation is of a *negative* nature, *omitting all interference* in the individual sphere, which is characteristic of the *negative freedom* of the nineteenth-century liberal state—according to which *everything is permitted except for that which is expressly prohibited*. The value that is protected in civil and political rights is, therefore, basically that of *individual freedom*, with the active subject par excellence of said rights being the *individual against society*.

Second generation rights contrast with the above mentioned rights since they are *gradual* rights, of a *moral* character, more than they are rights that are directly subject to judicial review. There are those that consider them as, more than authentic subjective rights, as *widespread interests*, since there is no corresponding organ that can directly demand their fulfillment. The key issue from this perspective is not so much the rights' formal recognition in legal texts—their *validity*—but rather their effective fulfillment on the factual level—their *effectiveness*. Unlike first generation rights, the second generation rights require *active* state participation when it comes time to supplying and providing for such rights. This should be done through *positive* state intervention—by giving *benefits or assistance*, and by promoting the rights' efficiency and removing obstacles that obstruct their abundance. This is typical of a social *Rechtstaat*, a system that is not satisfied with merely tolerating—*pati*—but rather intervenes—*facere*—with active behavior when necessary. The protected value is that of *equality*—understood as a real equality of opportunities, not as a mere formal equality. This true equality is meant to avoid that the laws of the strong produce a disproportional allocation of the wealth and exacerbate social inequalities. The active subject of these rights is the *citizen*, who should make sure these rights mean something *against the state*—more so than the individual against society, as the theories of the social contract put it, which distinguished between the state of nature and the state of civil society.[66]

4.2 *Third Generation Rights*

Third generation rights emerged in order to give a name, in the terminology of Karel Vasak, to the rights of *solidarity*.[67] Amongst those rights of particular note is the right of national self-determination (which relates to a topic which was already examined in this book: that of multiculturalism), the right to sustainable development or the right to peace (that for its special importance today I will deal with in a separate section). This third generation of rights is characterized by having an active subject that enjoys said rights in a *collective fashion*. It is not only the isolated individual or citizen, but rather groups or collectives such as the people, the nation, the society or humanity as a whole. The value that rules over these rights is that of *international solidarity*. And in a globalized world like the one we live in today, who can think of enjoying the right to peace or respecting the environment if it is not in cooperation with others? We cannot live in a world that is less contaminated unless the huge superpowers and the entire world support the common effort to fight for a healthier ecosystem. The same can be said regarding the right to peace. If a world conflict breaks out, would anyone be safe from danger? Isn't the danger of international terrorism a threat that can affect, that potentially does "affect," all of us?

66 See María José Falcón y Tella, "Las generaciones de derechos y la guerra," in the *Anuario de Derechos Humanos, Nueva Época*, vol. 4, 2003, Instituto de Derechos Humanos, Facultad de Derecho, Universidad Complutense de Madrid, pp. 35-55. Regarding social rights, see María José Añon Roig (*et al.*), *La universalidad de los derechos sociales: el reto de la inmigración*, Valencia, Universidad de Valencia, Servicio de Publicaciones, 1st edition, 1st reprint, 2004.

67 Karel Vasak, *Pour les droits de l'homme de la troisième génération*, Strasbourg, Institut International des Droits de l'Homme, 1979. *Id.* "Pour une troisième génération des droits de l'homme", in *Etudes et essais sur le droit international humanitaire et sur les principes de la Croix-Rouge en l'honneur de Jean Pictet*, La Haye, Mouton, 1984.

4.3 *Do Fourth Generation Rights Exist?*

This is, without a doubt, a good question. In reality if it is affirmed that fourth generation rights exist it is to mark a division between third generation rights and those rights that some doctrinal sectors already consider a fourth generation—a category that has a certain nature and specific characteristics. Those authors that have claimed that third generation rights have given way to a new dimension base their ideas on the existence of a *qualitative leap* between rights of solidarity and other categories that have recently emerged. These new categories have come about due to phenomena like the great developments in the area of biotechnology (with very conflictive issues such as the cloning of and experimenting with stem cells for therapeutic or reproductive purposes) or the Internet (and the problem of its regulation)—phenomena that only a few decades ago were unthinkable. There is no lack of reluctance, however, on the part of many theorists who prefer to continue embracing these new advances as part of the third generation of rights. There are others that simply prefer not to consider the issue as resolved, and who think that the guarantees of said rights are difficult to reach—an issue that links us to the subject of the implementation and effectiveness of human rights, especially those of the most recent generation.

4.3.1 The Problem of Its Implementation and Effectiveness

The problem of the implementation and effectiveness of human rights began to arise, as was already pointed out, with second generation rights, increased in the third generation, and increased even more so in the fourth generation. Regarding this notion of responsibility, for instance in the Spanish legal system, article 53 of the current Constitution points out that the guiding principles of the social and economic policy "will help serve as a guide in the creation of positive legislation, judicial practice and intervention by the public powers." Although the legal mandate refers to the three powers—legislative, executive and judicial—the Constitution says that they can only be legally responsible "in conformity with the laws that develop them." This seems to imply that the state is not directly responsible for political and civil rights. Nonetheless, in practice the three branches are often legally responsible, having recourse to the existence of a violation of the principle of real equality, which prohibits irrational discrimination.[68]

If the ability to bring second generation rights before judicial review is questionable, the issue is all the more arduous when it comes to third generation rights. Although it has already been pointed out that today there are institutions like the International Criminal Court that attempt to make progress in the implementation of human rights, it has also been emphasized that there is still a long way to go. The International Criminal Court has all sorts of obstacles and limits, which cause its effectiveness to be questioned. As a result the third generation rights that the Court protects are then also questioned—especially the right to peace and to universal justice.

4.3.2 Advances in Biomedicine

A The Problem Entailed by Cloning

In recent times bioethics have undergone enormous developments. Nonetheless, in the same manner as with the Internet, the new discoveries cause doubts to crop up regarding what certain new biological discoveries should be used for and under what circumstances. There also arises the need to guide the use of these discoveries by a moral code, so that abuses and dangers are avoided. Something that comes up right away when we consider these notions is the issue of experimenting with stem cells,[69] in particular the contro-

68 Regarding the subject, see Aniza Fernanda García Morales, *La justiciabilidad de..., op. cit.*, esp. pp. 125 ff. Extensively developed, and awarded with the first prize for legal essays—*Sapere Aude*, the 2003 edition—regarding the effectiveness of one of the most modern declarations of human rights, see Juan Francisco Moreno Domínguez, "La Carta de los Derechos Fundamentales de la Unión Europea: desde la solemnidad a la eficacia," in *Derecho y conocimiento*, vol. 2, pp. 325-347.

69 Regarding the subject of bioethics it is worth noting, among others, the following works of Professor José Miguel Serrano Ruiz-Calderón, "La guerra y la justificación de la muerte del inocente en el Mundo contemporáneo," in VV.AA., *Guerra, Moral y Derecho*, Madrid, Actas, pp. 71-

versial topic of whether an embryo can or cannot be considered a subject of human rights. "Personism" maintains the distinction between the concepts of the person—the subject of human rights, "the fetus that has a human figure and lives at least 24 hours after it has entirely parted with the womb," as article 30 of the Spanish Civil Code explains—and that of a human being, to the point that one could affirm that "*to kill human beings is wrong, but to kill persons is even worse*." This statement can be linked to others of a utilitarian tilt, such as those by Professor Peter Singer of Princeton University, who defends animal rights, and for whom there exist animals that have the same rights as persons and human beings that, if they are not persons, do not have such rights.

As such it is necessary to consider the issue of when life begins and, as a different issue, when we must begin protecting life. Responding to the first issue, Jesús Ballesteros responds (in a summer course in August, 2002, in El Escorial, directed by Professor José Iturmendi Morales[70]) that there already exists life in the embryo or in stem cells, but that not until birth is a legal personality acquired. Thus, an embryo, although it could not be considered a subject of rights, could be considered an object of protection, in the same fashion as a work of art. The German thinker Jürgen Habermas talks about a consumer science of embryos.[71] Others distinguish between

83. *Familia y Tecnología*, Madrid, Servicio de Publicaciones, Facultad de Derecho, Universidad Complutense de Madrid, 1996. *Eutanasia y vida dependiente. Inconvenientes jurídicos y consecuencias sociales de la despenalización de la eutanasia*, Madrid, Ediciones Internacionales Universitarias, 1st ed., January 2001.

70 See the chronical of the course given by Ana Valero Fernández de Palencia, published in the *Anuario de Derechos Humanos, Nueva Época*, Facultad de Derecho, Universidad Complutense de Madrid, vol. 3, pp. 561-590, esp. the portion given by Jesús Ballesteros. Also see volume 5, 2004, of said *Anuario*, pp. 215-241, esp. pp. 238-239, where the portion given by Ballesteros is referenced.

71 Jürgen Habermas, *El futuro de la naturaleza humana. ¿Hacia una eugenesia liberal?*, Spanish translation by R. S. Carbó, Barcelona, Paidós, 2002; reviewed by María Eugenia Pérez Montero, in the *Anuario de Derechos Humanos. Nueva Época*, Instituto de Derechos Humanos, Fa-

embryos and pre-embryos and, in relation to the controversial issue of cloning, between cloning with therapeutic ends or with reproductive ends, with the latter being clearly rejected.

B Biotechnologies and Privacy

Currently privacy is a right that is often-cited regarding the flow of information—including the consultation of, access to, correction of and cancellation of personal data that concern everyone who has fundamental rights—*habeas data*. Amongst this data there is one category of special importance,[72] to the point of considering such information particularly sensitive, which is data that reference people's health. With this in mind, it is valid to admit the existence of a right to information. Every citizen should have access to and control of their own clinical records that they compile from birth till death—biohealth *habeas data*.

Nowadays this information can be exhaustively processed, stored and transmitted thanks to developments in computer technology. But these technological advances can lead to violations of the right to privacy. This becomes a problem especially when it comes to data referencing contagious diseases or other diseases that can be used for making advancements in scientific research. In these and other situations there is tension between, on the one hand, the right to privacy and the desire to maintain respect for data that concerns citizens, and, on the other hand, the demands of medical research that need access to data contained in a multitude of clinical records. Sometimes such data can be used in an anonymous fashion, but on other occasions, for the research to be effective, the identities of the patients need to be revealed.

cultad de Derecho, Universidad Complutense de Madrid, vol. 4, 2003, pp. 437-444.

72 Other data that is especially protected by the Spanish Organic Law 15/1999, from December 13 (for the protection of data of a personal nature), to which I do not refer to in the present book, are personal data that reveal ideologies, union affiliations, religion and beliefs, personal data regarding racial origins and ones sex life, and personal data regarding ones criminal history.

From the different norms that regulate the topic, as much so in Spanish law[73] as in comparative law, there follow a series of principles relating to the matter:

- The principle of *sensitivity*: personal data dealing with health is considered sensitive data because it affects the core of personal privacy, and thus such data requires strengthened legal protection.
- The principle of *information and control.* Everyone should have the right to know and have access to as much information about their own health as is on record, and to exercise control over said information. They should also know why such information is on record and their consent must be required to make use of such information.
- The principle of *solidarity.* When it is an issue dealing with epidemiological and/or contagious diseases, there is a public interest to make use of and transmit personal data in order to prevent or eradicate such diseases.
- The principle of the *least amount of restriction possible.* In those cases in which the right to the privacy of personal health data must be restricted for reasons of solidarity, the restriction should be limited only to that which is absolutely necessary. Especially relevant to this issue are files that contain data re-

73 In Spain, Organic Law 15/1999 (for the protection of data of a personal nature), from December 13, requires express, written consent for the retrieval and treatment of personal data related to health, unless this action is legally authorized due to reasons of general interest. Nonetheless, article 7 permits the treatment of said data when it is necessary for precautionary medical procedures or a diagnostic exam, for providing health assistance, or for the management of health services, as long as the data is dealt with by a health-care professional that is subject to the rule of professional confidentiality. As an exception, the consent of the patient is not needed to gain access to their personal healthcare data when it is a necessary step to resolve an emergency or to carry out epidemiological studies.

lated to AIDS, since the personal data included in such files must necessarily be protected due to its private nature.[74]

4.3.3 The Problem of New Technologies

A The Problems Related to Internet Regulation

In this section we address an issue of great importance in today's world,[75] that being the impact of the Internet (*International Network of Computers*) in the realm of freedoms. It is a subject in which the guarantees of civil rights are put into conflict with the development of new technologies. The sphere of the Internet also includes data transfer networks that make it seem as though the size of the world has shrunk, that now there are no distances and that the citizenship today posses global dimensions, resulting in a shift from state borders to a cosmopolitan citizenship. The goal is to achieve technological advances that neither damage civic liberties nor are reached at the cost of such liberties.

The Internet has become the star phenomenon of new information and communication technologies which started to come into being in the early 1990s. Together with the unquestionable advantages and possibilities that the network of networks has made available in recent times, there are also serious causes for worry. Such problems linked to the Internet include the threat of phenomena like the trafficking of images of child prostitution, the spreading of neo-Nazi and terrorist groups' propaganda, the strengthening of

---

74 See, among others, Antonio-Enrique Pérez Luño, *La tercera generación de derechos humanos, op.cit.*, pp. 129-163. María Casado, *Bioética, Derecho y Sociedad*, Madrid, Trotta, 1998. Pablo Lucas Murillo de la Cueva, *El derecho a la autodeterminación informativa*, Madrid, Tecnos, 1990.

75 Regarding the subject see the works of a professor from our Department, Professor Emilio Suñé Llinás, "Introducción a la informática jurídica y al Derecho de la informática," in *Informática y Derecho, Revista de la Facultad de Derecho de la Universidad Complutense de Madrid*, 12, 1986, pp. 65-79. "Bases de datos normativas", in *Civitas. Revista Española de Derecho Administrativo*, 45, 1989, pp. 85-110. *Informática práctica para juristas y profesionales del mundo de las letras*, Madrid, Servicio de Publicaciones, Facultad de Derecho, Universidad Complutense de Madrid, 1994.

viruses and the entering of systems by so-called computer pirates (*hackers*), or the violation of the protection of personal data. Such situations can threaten basic legal rights, such as those regarding privacy, public image, people's dignity and honor, sexual freedom, intellectual and industrial property, the free market, consumer protection, national security and public order.

In addition to these problems there is the difficulty of finding, preventing and punishing these actions, given their international and unlimited nature which can bring about conflicts regarding the correct location of the competent sanctioning body. The French doctrine speaks of a "*délocalisation*" of the Internet, stressing how difficult it is to know what laws are applicable to actions that are carried out through a global network that has no precise geographic location. What's more, it is difficult to know if those who should be held responsible are the *creators* of the illegal information, those that facilitate the access to and *transmission* of this information, or the *consumers* that use such information. In addition, one must also consider the fact that often, since it is an issue of new types of crime, there exist old legal categories that are part of legal norms which are not fully appropriate and adaptable. As a result there arises the problem of legal gaps, which are not always due to negligence by the legislature. These gaps lead to a kind of impunity for such criminal acts. Due to all of the aforementioned, it is difficult to discover, prove and pursue this type of Internet-related crime.

To combat the new risks created by the Internet, there are new security measures that attempt to alleviate those risks. This is the case of "*encryption programs*," that transform natural language messages into coded messages, thus making them unreadable for all those who do not have the key to decode the message. The encryption program PGP (*Pretty Good Privacy*), for instance, is well-known due to Philip Zimmermann. On the flipside, however, these programs have contributed to making it more difficult to discover illegal information networks. Other security measures are: "*filters*," which consist of selected computer programs that block access to determined documents; "*firewalls*," that facilitate or impede the transfer of images or data from the Internet to a computer or vice versa; "*digital certificates*," that permit one to identify or connect to all the parts that control commercial transactions through the Internet, making them fast and safe; and the "*cyberpolice*," which are entities that offer teams of experts that specialize in the localization of Internet pirates and provide defense programs against sabotage.[76]

On the other hand, to combat these new forms of crime fostered by the Web, strong national security systems have been created, such as *Echelon* and *Carnivore*. These systems make possible world-wide surveillance of communications by satellite and allow one to catch and learn the content of all messages sent by fax, telephone, Internet or e-mail, regardless of the sender. This ability entails a worrisome risk for civic liberties, posing the dilemma of "security *versus* freedom." Said ability could also lead to uncontrolled surveillance of millions of citizens of all the countries of the world, using the terrible attacks of September 11, 2001 as an excuse. The potential for this sort of surveillance spreads the notion of *an eye of God*, in a kind of "*Big Brother*"—a figure that George Orwell used to designate what, in his judgment, would happen in 1984 when a totalitarian and omnipresent state that sees all would reign. Such surveillance would impede crimes, which could one day cease to exist, but would also infringe on freedoms.

In his work *The Spirit of the Laws*, Montesquieu pointed out that in all, or almost all European governments, punishment has grown or diminished in proportion with how much the government favored or discouraged freedom. Severe punishments were common in despotic governments—which were based on terror—more than in the monarchy or in democracy—which were based on honor and civil virtue. Almost a century later, Alexis de Tocqueville affirmed that "*although the society of the United States of America is a paradigmatic example of liberty, the prisons of said country offer a view of the most despotic*."[77] The facts of which Montesquieu and

76 Relating to the topic, see Nuria Cuadrado Gamarra, *Aplicación de los sistemas expertos al campo del Derecho*, Prologue by Emilio Suñé Llinás, Servicio de Publicaciones, Facultad de Derecho, Universidad Complutense de Madrid, 2004.

77 Gustav de Beaumont and Alexis de Tocqueville, *On the Penitentiary System in the United States*, Philadelphia, 1833, p. 47.

De Tocqueville spoke of continue to be debated and investigated today.

Émile Durkheim puts great emphasis on marking the *limits between psychology and sociology* in relation to crime. Crime from a psychological point of view can be a *pathological* phenomenon. However, according to Durkheim's sociology, crime is a *normal* social phenomenon. Durkheim makes use of an uncommon concept of normality, a concept that simple common sense seems to indicate. In sociology the normality of a fact is determined by whether said fact is something that is *generally* present in a certain type of society in one phase of its development. Considering that crimes are part of a phenomena that has been present in societies from every age and place, and that crime is not something that diminishes with the onset of civilization, but rather it grows with it, one can conclude that from a sociological standpoint crime is something normal in all of society. There is only one limit regarding the normality of crime: that it does not cause a break in the *social equilibrium* where, according to Durkheim, the health of society lies. The idea of social equilibrium, which is considered essential, depends on *flexibility*: a system must be sufficiently flexible to permit a certain level of crime. When the number of crimes *is not out of control*, society does not run a serious danger, and is not thrown off balance. What's more, deviant behavior has the mark of something personal, of something *original*, and in this way is similar to a creative or heroic act. For heroism and creativity to be produced in society, a certain level of *freedom* must be permitted—a certain margin to disobey the rules. The other side of the coin of this freedom is crime. The ideal situation is a *middle-ground* between obedience and regularity, on the one hand, and dissension and originality, on the other. It is best not to deviate from the norm, not to break the equilibrium, either by having too little or too much of something.

Durkheim distinguishes between *the moral and the sociological* when considering crime, by not only considering crime a normal social fact, but also considering it a *positive* social fact. Although psychology views crime as an indication of pathology, and although from a moral standpoint it deserves to be reproached, for sociology if it does not cause a social imbalance—which is to say, if it is

maintained within the limits of reasonable quantities—then crime fulfills a positive social function. It is a positive function insofar as it shows the health of society by being an expression of freedom and creativity, although in their negative form. Durkheim's thesis is one of reformulation, in sociological terms, of the *theological problem of good and evil: good is only possible if evil is also possible.* The reason is simple: good and evil presuppose freedom. Without freedom one could not do evil, but one could also not do good. They are two sides of the same coin. Together with this *indirect* usefulness, crime also has in certain cases a *direct* usefulness: crime can be useful in *directly preparing us for social changes, anticipating the morality of the future.* This was what happened with *Socrates*, who was ahead of his time, and defended freedom of expression despite the fact that this led to his death sentence in accordance with the Athenian laws. This was also the situation of *Jesus Christ*, who died on the cross, convicted as a common criminal according to the laws of the time, but who also planted a message of brotherly love for future generations.[78]

Leaving behind this *excursus* dealing with freedom and crime, and returning to the subject of the Internet and cyberspace, the dilemma arises between *libertarian anarchy* and *guaranteed freedom*. One should not back down from the risks of a criminal *invasion* by people who spy on others that navigate the Web, or from the *colonization* of cyberspace by state powers, with the consequent limitations on freedom. These risks relate to the subject of Internet regulation. In its beginnings the Web was an "anarchistic" space, totally free from all control or authority that could have regulated it. An example of this anarchic and libertarian conception is the Declaration of Independence of Cyberspace, proclaimed in Davos, Switzerland on February 8, 1996. This declaration revolved around three main points: the total autonomy of the cybernauts—"governments of the industrial world...are not welcome among us"; the inapplicability of traditional concepts and categories, based on the portion of the declaration that states, "...but in our world the mate-

78 Gregorio Robles Morchón, *Crimen y castigo (Ensayo sobre Durkheim)*, Madrid, Civitas, 2001, pp. 73-83.

rial does not exist"; and the idyllic and utopian vision of cyberspace as a space that does not need state regulation.

As a counterpoint to this idyllic vision, other authors point out the great inequalities that have originated from the Internet. These inequalities have permitted the distinction between the *info-rich* and the *info-poor*, emphasizing the North-South split. For instance, there are more telephone lines on Manhattan Island, New York, than in all of black Africa. This causes Ignacio Ramonet to exclaim that: "the Internet was hope; that hope has been stolen."[79] Paradoxically, the main beneficiaries of the anarchy and absence of Internet regulation are not the individual cybernauts, but rather huge multinationals.

The Internet is too complex of a phenomenon to be able to be regulated by only one specific norm, since it affects multiple branches of the legal order. In Spain, the first norm that serves as the center or axis of attention and analysis of the Web is Law 34/2002, from July 11, of Services of the Information Society and of Electronic Commerce. Technically the law does not regulate the Web as such, since its object is the regulation of the legal regimen of the information society and the regulation of recruitment/hiring through electronic means. Said law incorporates into the Spanish legal order Directive 2000/31/CE of the European Parliament and European Council from June 8 (Directive over electronic commerce), relative to certain legal aspects of information society services, in particular electronic commerce in the internal market.[80]

In Spain there has also been an attempt to give a legal answer to the issue of the Internet by invoking articles 186 and 301 of the Spanish Penal Code of 1995. But the articles deal with types of crimi-

79 Ignacio Ramonet, "¡Nos han robado la esperanza!", in "Internet, ¿un bien o una maldición?", in *El País Digital-Debates*, 25 February 1997.

80 Published in the Official Diary of European Communities number 178, from July 17, 2000. The topic of globalization, examined in this book, is intimately related to the Internet, as is reflected by the work of Javier Barraca Mairal (*et al.*); Francisco J. Roa (comp.), *Globalización, Internet y marketing: una respuesta ética*, Murcia, Universidad Católica San Antonio, 2003.

nal activity that have nothing to do with Internet crimes. As a result there have been other attempts to create new criminal categories that are more suitable to the new virtual reality. Following this train of thought, the United States Congress passed in February, 1996 the *Communications Decency Act*—CDA—a norm that, nonetheless, has been very controversial and at the center of various appeals aimed at declaring it unconstitutional—for going against the First Amendment of the U.S. Constitution by establishing a type of prior censorship; as well as violating guarantees under the due process of law, recognized by the Fifth Amendment. In the heart of the European Union the first important norm related to the topic was *Directive 95/46*. Also, in October 1996 the European Commission issued a Communication on *illegal and harmful content on the Internet*. This initiative is complemented by the *Green Paper on the protection of minors and human dignity in audiovisual and information services*. Another legal effort to fight Internet crime can be seen in the *European Human Rights Convention* (arts. 8 and 10.2) and the *Charter of Fundamental Rights of the European Union* proclaimed in Nice on December, 2000 (especially in its articles 8 and 54). The idea is not to impose restrictions on the freedom of audiovisual expression that are not justified by the test of proportionality. In European jurisprudence it is worth noting the sentence of the European Court of Justice from November 6, 2003 (issue C-101/01), in the so-called *Lindqvist case*.

On the whole, it is necessary to find an equilibrium between the Internet and civil rights. Regarding the strengthening of civil rights through the Internet, there are basically two positions that respond to opposing visions of the problem. On one hand are the *critical positions*, represented in the book *Republic.com* by the American author Cass Sunstein.[81] Sunstein believes that the Web fosters a type of *individualized* political communication that makes collective political programs difficult. The Internet has generated, according to this author, individual habits of an *egotistical* nature, that only search out things for one's own use and benefit. This style

81 Cass Sunstein, *Republic.com*, Princeton, Princeton University Press, 2001; Spanish translation by P. García Segura, Barcelona, Paidós, 2003.

goes against the supportive attitude that should preside over political action. What's more, cybernauts become the *passive consumers* of programs generated by great economic powers, which conflicts with the active citizenship of the political man. According to Sunstein, we are experiencing a *republic.com* of subjects more so than of actual citizens.

Opposing Sunstein's point of view, the optimistic version of the issue is known under the title of "*cyber-republic*," which entails a responsible, active, committed, free and egalitarian community that goes beyond state monopolies. If borders cannot be put up in mid-air and would not hold anyone back anyway since there are no customs offices in the sky,[82] then it also would make no sense to erect monopolistic or oligarchic walls, customs offices and tolls in cyberspace. Examples of a responsible and united electronic citizenry, or "*cyber-republic*," are statements by cybernauts opposing the stoning of women in Nigeria or, amongst other issues, protesting the military intervention in Iraq.

The middle ground, an alternative that lies between the positive dimension, the cyber-republic, and the negative, evoked by *republic.com*,[83] is illustrated in the title of the work of Umberto Eco, *Apocalittici e integrati*. There exist, according to this Italian author, apocalyptic thinkers that pursue a fatalistic train of thought and are guided by pessimism—amongst these authors are George Orwell,[84] in his celebrated novel *1984*, Robert Musil[85] or Herbert Marcuse.[86] On the other hand are those that are integrated, a term that designates the most optimistic. As a name for these types of subjects,

82 This air metaphor comes from Martha Nussbaum, *Los límites del patriotismo. Identidad, pertenencia y "ciudadanía mundial,"* Spanish translation by C. Castells, Barcelona, Paidós, 1999.

83 See Antonio-Enrique Pérez Luño, *¿Ciberciudadanía@ o ciudadanía@ com?*, Barcelona, Gedisa, 2004.

84 George Orwell, *1984*, Barcelona, Destino, 5th ed., 1980.

85 Robert Musil, *Der Mann ohne Eigenschaften*, Hamburg, Rowohlt, 1952.

86 Herbert Marcuse, *One-Dimensional Man. Studies in the Ideology of Advanced Industrial Society*, London, Routledge & Kegan Paul, 1964.

Henri Lefèbvre has proposed the term "*cybernanthrope*"—the *cybernetic* man, who lives in symbiosis with machine.[87]

There is no doubt that there must be a tendency towards establishing a cyberspatial legal ethic. In the French-speaking world they have used the expression "*Netiquette*," which is to say an ethic of the Net, to allude to the deontological rules that should preside over the use of the Internet.[88]

B The So-called "Electronic Civil Disobedience" as a Newly Appearing Phenomenon

What action can one take against an unjust law? What value should win out in the case of a conflict between the legal order and the natural order: the positive law or the moral law? This is the eternal dilemma that thousands of people have confronted throughout the history of humanity. In reality, as Oscar Wilde once put it: "*two human beings cannot be together half an hour without one acquiring a*

---

87 Henri Lefèbvre, *Vers le cybernanthrope*, Paris, Denoël & Gonthier, 2000.

88 Regarding this development I have followed, among others, Antonio-Enrique Pérez Luño, *La tercera generación de derechos humanos, op.cit.*, pp. 87-129. *Id. Manual de Informática y Derecho*, Barcelona, Ariel, 1996; Vittorio Frosini, *Law and Liberty in the Computer Age*, Oslo, Tano, 1995; *Id. La democracia nel XXI secolo*, Roma, Ideazione, 1997; *Id., L'uomo artificiale. Etica e diritto nell'era planetaria*, Milano, Spirali, 1986. Teresa García-Berrio, *Informática y libertades. La protección de datos personales y su regulación en Francia y España*, Murcia, Servicio de Publicaciones de la Universidad de Murcia, 2003. A. Garriga Domínguez, *La protección de los datos personales en el Derecho español*, prologue by Antonio-Enrique Pérez Luño, Madrid, Universidad Carlos III & Dykinson, 1999; *Id. Tratamiento de datos personales y derechos fundamentales*, Madrid, Dykinson, 2004. Ernesto Garzón Valdés, "Optimismo y pesimismo en la democracia," in *Claves de Razón Práctica*, 131, 2003. D. Lagares, *Internet y el Derecho*, Barcelona, Ediciones Carena, 2nd ed., 2000. Mario G. Losano, *Corso di Informatica giuridica, vol. I, Informatica per le scienze sociali*, Torino, Einaudi, 1985; *vol. II, 1, Il diritto privatto dell'informatica*, Torino, Einaudi, 1986; *vol. II. 2, Il diritto pubblico dell'informatica*, Torino, Einaudi, 1986. Giovanni Sartori, *Homo videns. La sociedad teledirigida*, Madrid, Taurus, 1998.

notable superiority over the other" and *"wherever there is a man who exercises authority, there is a man who resists authority."* The characters of Lucifer, Antigone, Socrates,[89] Jesus Christ and many others who were disobedient show that sometimes the following philosophy is lawful and just: *if you can't change things, at least make sure that things don't change you.*[90]

Nonetheless, although the phenomenon of disobeying unjust laws is ancient, it was not until the middle of the 19th century that the term was coined, in the work of the American thinker Henry David Thoreau, in reality due to the initiative of his editor who published the work posthumously with the title of *On Civil Disobedience.* From there we can move on to Gandhi in India—who spoke of the *Satyagraha* or "triumph of the truth"—and to Martin Luther King in the U.S. In America there is a greater frequency of civil disobedience than in Europe, where revolutions tend to predominate more than dissent within the system itself. In the United States the phenomenon became very well-known in the pro-civil rights movements of the 1960s—e.g. the suffrage movement, Labor Movement,

89 Regarding the topic of Socrates, I want to highlight here the work of José Iturmendi Morales, "Proceso y muerte de Sócrates. Un sabio ante la justicia de su tiempo", en *Grandes abogados, grandes procesos que hicieron historia,* Pamplona, Aranzadi, 1997, pp. 155-159.

90 Regarding the topic, María José Falcón y Tella, *La desobediencia civil,* prologue by Fernando Garrido Falla, Madrid, Marcial Pons, 2000. There is an English translation by Peter Muckley, of the first part, *Civil Disobedience,* prologue by Martti Koskenniemi, Boston-Leiden, Martinus Nijhoff Publishers, 2004; and of the second part, *A History of Civil Disobedience,* Genève, Editions Diversités, 2004. Reviewed by Guido Saraceni, in the *Rivista Internazionale di Filosofia del Diritto,* 3, 2001, pp. 424-426; by Paula López Zamora, in the *Revista de Estudios Políticos,* 111, pp. 312-314; by Beatriz Castro Toledo, in the *Revista de la Facultad de Derecho de la Universidad Complutense de Madrid,* 2001, pp. 241-263; by Oscar Mª Prieto García, in the *Anuario de Derechos Humanos, Nueva Época,* vol. 2, Instituto de Derechos Humanos, Facultad de Derecho, Universidad Complutense de Madrid, 2001, pp. 1026-1035; by Juan Antonio Martínez Muñoz, in *Siglo Veintiuno, Revista de Pensamiento y Cultura,* 53, Spring 2002, pp. 146-148; and by Pedro Rivas, "De nuevo sobre la desobediencia civil," in *Anales de la Cátedra Francisco Suárez,* 34, 2000, pp. 447-450.

etc. Civil disobedience is also an important part of the anti-war movement. Some examples include student protests against the Vietnam War, the struggle of the Berrigan brothers, amongst others, and other movements such as that of *tax resistance* (the refusal to pay taxes when they help finance an unjust war—following in the finest traditions of Thoreau) or *nuclear resistance* (against the arms race and nuclear testing). In Europe, civil disobedience has occurred occasionally, such as with the peaceful campaigns of Bertrand Russell in Great Britain, the movement of refusing to do military service or community service in Spain before a professional army existed, or the actions of Dnilo Dolci in Italy, among others.

It is not this type of "classic" civil disobedience, however, that I want to refer to here, but rather something novel that emerges from the aforementioned. I am referring to the so-called *electronic civil disobedience*, a phenomenon that has recently appeared that, although not yet well-defined, refers to disobedience on the Net that makes use of the resources and advances that such technology permits.

Next, I will expand on the description this phenomenon, referring to some of the modern tactics that the movement incorporates. Everyone knows that the Net, the Internet to be exact, has allowed for great progress in all fields, opening an unimaginable fan of possibilities for different actions. But the Net also involves dangers, which is why there are many people who advocate complete Internet regulation.[91] But, where does electronic civil disobedience fit into all this? As a quasi-legal phenomenon, should one be punished as if it were an ordinary case of disobedience? How does one electronically "disobey" the law?

Some examples of electronic civil disobedience would be: collapsing Web pages so that no one can access them; or so-called "cyber-graffiti," when through a word in a search-engine like *Google*, direct "access" appears to a specific Web page; or when campaigns of civil disobedience are called together through the Web—a method typically used by Zapatismo in Chiapas; or when domain names are created that are very similar to ones that already exist, having

91 *Vid.*, relating to this topic, section II. 4. 3. 3. of this book.

as their only purpose the promotion of confusion and false identifications; or so-called *hacktivism*. It is necessary to distinguish between *hackers* (those that, for instance, get around filters on Webpages whose access is prohibited in a certain country) and *crackers* (electronic pirates that use the Web to get revenge for being fired unfairly or to embezzle money). Other Internet campaigns of civil disobedience are *anti-copyright movements*, which infringe on authors' rights—the rights that belong to the creators of an intellectual work and their heirs for a certain time period. This relates just as much to such authors' economic rights—a percentage of the sales—as to their moral rights—that their name appears, if it is not an anonymous work, or that their work is not plagiarized. Regarding this point it is necessary to point out that the electronic reproduction of classic books, like *Don Quixote* or *Crime and Punishment*, is permitted. What are not free, however, and have a fee due to copyright laws, are the notes of these works. Another problem with copyrights comes about with translations. Finally I will refer to, although only to point out the problem, civil disobedience relating to *cryptography*—the process used to encode messages. These encoded messages are like postcards in an envelope—you know you have a message, but you don't know what it says unless you are able to decrypt it by having the code. There are countries that prohibit all manner of cryptography (e.g. China), and it is then that the skilled Internet user is able to export these types of systems, violating the prohibition.

5 The Right to Peace and War Conflicts at Present

Peacefulness to the extreme is nice in theory, but unrealistic in practice. There are opposing theories about the character of human nature. For some, like Jean-Jacques Rousseau, man is good by nature and evil is the consequence of culture. Others, like John Hobbes, argue that there exists a seed of evil in all human beings from their birth, and that man is a wolf to man *—homo homini lupus*. Leaving this controversy aside for the moment, what does seem undeniable is that human beings—at the individual level—and states—on the international level—occasionally enter into conflicts with each other, and the strongest subjugate the weakest. It is for this reason that law on occasion must permit states to conduct actions in the international sphere that are punished if they are committed within the country. As is popularly said, although it seems contradictory, many times "battles are fought with the sole purpose of putting an end to war," or that "frequently it is only possible to guarantee peace with violence."

Due to the aforementioned, recourse to a certain level of *controlled* violence by way of the legitimate defense of the *status quo*, to avoid that an aggressor *gets his own way*, would be justified in principle in some situations. That is why international law has come to legitimize so-called defensive wars. But after the sadly famous and tragic events of September 11, 2001 in New York and Washington, international law has experienced a serious shift in its stance by admitting for the first time as legitimate—although this has been continually questioned by many legal internationalists and theorists—so-called *preventive* wars, or wars of anticipation.[92]

5.1 The Evolution of the Conception of War after 9/11: From "Defensive" War to "Preventive" War

It would be very easy to take the position that we should always reject war—and it is, because everyone knows the great destructive potential that war holds at all levels, and the great human desolation and physical devastation that it entails. Nobody, except a sadist or a psychopath, enjoys killing—and war is nothing but a great slaughter. But this analysis would be excessively simplistic if one did not specify and distinguish between different types of war. Simply put, not all wars are the same. For now we will leave aside the

92 An example of preventive war is the recent war in Iraq (although it still continues openly), because the difficult part is not so much militarily defeating a country, but rather erecting the pillars of a lasting peace. There have been many authors that have opposed the Iraqi war. Regarding the subject, it is worth highlighting Milan Rai, *Plan de guerra contra Irak: diez razones para no iniciar una nueva guerra contra Irak;* with a capital by Noam Chomsky, Spanish translation by Juan Mari Madariaga, edition of Carlos Prieto del Campo, Madrid, Foca, 2003.

complex typology of wars, which permits us to distinguish an endless number of varieties: fratricides, civil wars, wars of succession, wars of annexation, guerrilla wars, atomic wars, bacteriological wars, subversive wars,[93] and so on. Rather than this typology, what interests us here are cases of wars that are explainable (on the factual level), legal (in accordance with the norms and uses that should preside over all war conflicts, on a normative level), and in some cases perhaps justifiable (on a values level). Even if wars have these qualities, that does not change the fact that they are monstrous and must be the last recourse employed—only once all the diplomatic channels for the peaceful resolution of a controversy have been exhausted.[94]

Regarding this last point one can speak of "explainable," "excusable" and/or "justifiable" wars. The guidelines that mark whether we are experiencing one situation or another, however, are not the same today as they were in other eras. In this area there has been an evolution of international law—which regulates war as an international phenomenon and serves as the most important part of these humble reflections —from the classic concept of war to war in present times. The turning point that marks the passage from one

93 Talking about the topic of war in current times, see José de la Torre Martínez, "La guerra subversiva o revolucionaria," in VV.AA., *Guerra, Moral y Derecho*, Madrid, Actas, pp. 137-161, esp. p. 137: "*Within the numerous wars that are offered by the typology of bellicose conflicts appears one that, in current times, has acquired such a notable boom that it has become deserving of more and more attention by war scholars. We are referring to 'subversive war' or 'revolutionary war.' As Mr. Leandro Rubio García points out, "when presented with the discovery of the horror of thermonuclear war—and its improbability—one should not stop considering a much realer type of war: the revolutionary, subversive war.' It is a new kind of war characteristic of the 'iron age' in which we are immersed."* In the same collective volume, Juan Antonio Martínez Muñoz, "Guerra y Derecho internacional," pp. 85-109.

94 Regarding all-out war, see Michel Collon, *La guerra global ha comenzado*. Noam Chomsky, *La nueva guerra contra el terror.* James Petras, *Los intelectuales y la guerra: de la retirada a la rendición.* Fidel Castro (1926), *El terrorismo, la guerra y la crisis económica*, Hondarribia, Guipúzcoa, Hiru, 3rd ed., 2002.

conception of war to another is especially present on one historical date: September 11, 2001. Since that moment, there begins to be a considerable change in the various aspects of the uses and practices of war. These aspects were affected just as much regarding *jus ad bellum* (the right to declare war) as regarding *jus in bello* (the norms or rules that regulate practices during war).

The first new aspect in this evolution, which was referenced earlier, is the passage from *defensive* wars (the only legitimate type of war in classic international law) to the recent *preventive* wars or wars of *anticipation*. Currently there exists the peculiarity of trying to theoretically justify these preventive wars using the excuse that they are inevitable if we want to preserve the beloved international security, especially from the dangers of international terrorism—even though such protection involves the violation of rights valued by a hundred-years old tradition. It is not an issue of bringing back the *status quo* after an invasion or interference in state territory by outside forces (which is the definition of a classic defensive war), but rather of anticipating future events—making, or better said, trying to make good on the saying that "*the end justifies the means*."

Another difference I want to point out is that for years, during the "Cold War" (the bipolar situation produced after the end of World War II), each of the two blocks were in competition—with the U.S. and U.S.S.R. at the head of each block—to stockpile as many nuclear weapons as possible in order to dissuade the other side from starting war. The potential for a universal massacre had the effect of preventing a war from breaking out. It was the era of *armed peace*: "*if you want peace, prepare for war*." Today the situation is just the opposite: it is the *peaceful war* that is being fought. While bombs are dropped, so to are food and medicine, with the humanitarian purpose of alleviating the effects of the disaster. The humanitarian aid is carried out during the conflict, and not after as was done in the past, such as with the Marshall Plan.

The third aspect that distinguishes the situation before 9/11 from the current one is that in the past, when war occurred, it was *all-out* war. Hiroshima and Nagasaki show up to what point atomic bombs, and in reality all bombs, do not distinguish between civilians and soldiers or between combatants and non-combatants. Today, however, authors speak of wars *with a scalpel* or *surgical* wars, which remove the bad wherever it is, as if it were a tumor, leaving the social body as a whole alive. This attempt to minimize collateral damage is very praiseworthy in theory, but is unrealistic in its practical execution, as was made clear in the last offensive against Iraq.

Finally, I want to highlight that the *hostage*, as a classic figure that was exchanged for peace, today is replaced by a new figure, that of *human shields*. These human shields consist of people that, due to their mere presence in a country at war, diminish the possibility of an attack.[95]

5.2 Is It Possible to Speak of a "Just War"?

At this point I will refer to what many consider to be the central theme within this subject matter, which is the possibility or impossibility of a just war. The so-called theory of just war was first outlined by Cicero, St. Augustine, and at a later in time, by some authors of the Spanish theological school of the 17th century, like Francisco Suárez, Francisco de Vitoria, Domingo de Soto or the great tyrannicide theorist from our country, Juan de Mariana.

According to the theory, the theoretical requirements necessary to speak of the existence of a just war are:

1 *The cause must be a just one.* One must not confuse the "cause" with the motive, or "excuse," for entering a conflict, nor confuse the official cause with the real causes, which could be economic or strategic interests. As a result, the causes often are not clearly apparent or are not revealed to the public—which relates to what was discussed at the beginning of this book about the ways in which the media can manipulate such information.

95 Regarding the topic of the differences between classic war and bellicose conflicts in present times, see María José Falcón y Tella, *El ciudadano frente a la ley*, Buenos Aires-Madrid, Editorial Ciudad Argentina-Universidad Complutense de Madrid, 2004, esp. pp. 203-217. 2nd ed. 2006.

2 *War must be the last resort.* All other diplomatic channels available to negotiate a peaceful solution to the conflict must be exhausted first.

3 *War must be declared by the competent public authority.* In this situation I am referring to *jus ad bellum*. In the case of Vietnam, for instance, there was no formal declaration of war by the U.S. Congress, which in a way was "left aside" because the executive did not want to "wait." Maneuvers like these lead to belligerent interventions that "unilaterally move" the events forward.

4 *The government's intention to get involved in a war must not be related to hate, cruelty or the desire for revenge.* Although it is valid to admit that in the situation of a country that is attacked, in which there is disastrous poverty and human rights are not respected, and in which oftentimes the events that led to and pressured the country into the armed intervention are still fresh in people's minds, it is hard to totally separate the desire for revenge from the subsequent belligerent actions.

5 *There must exist a reasonable expectation of victory.* Once again, reality often contradicts the predicted outcomes of some wars. Given the military supremacy of the attackers, they often expect rapid offensives that will wrap up nicely. The fact is, however, that the abundance of deaths on both sides often rises to unimaginable proportions not only during the conflict, but also a great deal when the conflict ends and it is time to work towards peace and the country's reconstruction. Thus, no one knows if the *a posteriori* expectation of victory is as reasonable as it may seem at first glance.

6 *The positive achievements the military forces hope to reach must not be disproportionate to the collateral damage caused.* What was pointed out in the previous point is equally applicable here. It is true that sometimes belligerent interventions can be justified because the country which is attacked lived immersed in tyranny and there was enormous abuse of the civil population by the country's leaders, but one must consider if the new situation will be much better for the inhabitants. Was war the best solution? Were there other channels that could

have been explored? What has been the result of all this? These are all questions that must be considered before embarking on a war.

7 *The methods employed in the course of the war must be valid,* complying with the already-established *jus in bello.* Today we hear of surgical wars, but beyond the inevitable damage that occurs in all armed conflict—the unintentional deaths of women, children and a large number of non-combatants—that seems to some extent inevitable, what can and should be avoided are human rights violations, which shock the conscience of the civilized world. Also condemnable are some acts which, despite being contrary to the "uses of war," are nonetheless used as a way to pressure the enemy. Such actions go against the guidelines established by the Geneva Conventions regarding the treatment of prisoners of war.

5.3 *Terrorism and the "War on Terror"*

5.3.1 An Explanation on the Subject of International Terrorism in the World Today

In this book there was a section dedicated to the theme of globalization.[96] Clearly globalization is a highly relevant issue, considering that it even affects the subject of this section: terrorism.[97] In fact,

96 Regarding the topic of terrorism as a global phenomenon, see Felipe González Márquez, "Globalización del terror", in Ahmed Rashid *(et al.), El mundo después del 11 de septiembre de 2001*, Barcelona, Península, 2002, pp. 47-51. Fernando, Reinares, *Terrorismo global*, Madrid, Taurus, 2003. By the same author, also regarding the subject, *Terrorismo y antiterrorismo*, Barcelona, Paidós, 1998.

97 Regarding terrorism, see Montserrat Bordes Solanas, *El terrorismo: una lectura analítica*, Barcelona, Ediciones Bellaterra, 2000. Walter Laquear (1921-), *Terrorismo*, Spanish translation by José Luis López Muñoz, Madrid, Espasa-Calpe, 1980. And Robert H. Kupperman (1935-) – Darrell M. Trent, *Terrorismo: minaccia, realtá, difesa*, prologue by Walter Laquear, Roma, Bulzoni, 1981. Noel O'Sullivan (*et al.*), *Terrorismo, ideología y revolución*, Spanish tranlsation by Néstor A. Míguez, Madrid, Alianza, 1987. Terrorism is a phenomenon that has been growing a great deal since the

there are many kinds of terrorism,[98] such as nationalist terrorism,[99]

---

beginning of the 1970s within democratic systems and within the rule of law, as is reflected in a book by Carlos Horacio Domínguez, *El terrorismo en el Estado de Derecho*, prologue by Osiris G. Villegas, Buenos Aires, Abaco de Rodolfo Depalma, 1983. And a book by Salvador Giner (et al.); Fernando Reinares-Nestares (comp.), *Terrorismo y sociedad democrática*, Madrid, Akal, 1982. Regarding the legal treatment of terrorism, see José García San Pedro, *Terrorismo: aspectos criminológicos y legales*, Madrid, Universidad Complutense, Facultad de Derecho – Ministerio de Justicia. Centro de Estudios Jurídicos, 1993. And in the European legal field, Diego López Garrido, *Terrorismo, política y derecho: la legislación antiterrorista en España, Reino Unido, República Federal de Alemania, Italia y Francia*, Madrid, Alianza, 1987.

98 Movements that are often of a nationalistic or religious nature—such as the ETA and GRAPO in Spain, Direct Action in France, the Red Brigades in Italy, the IRA in Northern Ireland, the Red Army Faction in Germany, cells of communist combatants in Belgium, the Kurdish independence movement or some Arab organizations—that since the last third of the 20th century have afflicted certain countries, should be differentiated from the anarchistic terrorism from the last third of the 19th century. Regarding the latter type of terrorism, the anarchistic, see the study by Rafael Nuñez Florencio, *El terrorismo anarquista: (1888-1909)*, Madrid, Siglo Veintiuno, 1983.

99 Terrorism and nationalism is dealt with in Paul Gilbert, *Terrorismo, nacionalismo, pacificación*, introduction by Manuel Garrido, Spanish translation by Marco Aurelio Galmantini, Madrid, Ediciones Cátedra, 1998. Regarding nationalist terrorism, it is worth describing the kind that currently exists in our country. About this subject, see Alejandro Muñoz Alonso, *El terrorismo en España*, Barcelona, Planeta, 1982. Juan Terradillos Basoco, *Terrorismo y derecho: comentario a las leyes orgánicas 3 y 4-1988, de reforma del Código Penal y de la Ley de Enjuiciamiento Criminal*, Madrid, Tecnos, 1988. *Terrorismo*, Madrid, Ministerio de Defensa, Centro Superior de Información de la Defensa, 1979. Regarding the terrorist situation in Spain after the March 11, 2004 attacks, see Edurne Uriarte, *Terrorismo y democracia tras el 11-M*, Madrid, Espasa Calpe, 2004. In relation to other geographical contexts, see Eduardo González Calleja, *El terrorismo en Europa*, Madrid, Arco Libros, 2002. Arnold Joseph Toynbee (1889-1975), *El terrorismo alemán en Bélgica: narración basada en los documentos*, introduction by Ramiro de Maeztu, London, Hayman, Christy & Lilly, 1917.

religious terrorism[100] or a wide range of other types.[101] But right now what is especially worrisome is international terrorism,[102] fundamentally inspired by Islam, which provoked the tragic events pointed out earlier—events that may be considered by future historians as marking the passage into a new historical era. It is a type of terrorism that functions as a *global network*, in a decentralized fashion without just one base of operations. This type of terrorism does not distinguish

100 Regarding the growing expansion and boom in terrorism of a religious nature, it is worth highlighting Mark Juergensmeyer, *Terrorismo religioso: el auge global de la violencia religiosa*, Madrid, Siglo XXI, 2001.

101 As one type of terrorism, leftist terrorism is studied in Donatella Della Porta (1956-), *Il terrorismo di sinistra*, Bologna, Il Mulino, 1990. Speaking on acidic terrorism, Roberto Ferlicca, *Terrorismo ácido*, Milano, Greco & Greco, 1991. There are those who have coined the terminology "terrorism of the state," to refer to actions perpetrated by a state's very own political powers. Regarding this subject, Jorge A. Tapia Valdés, *El terrorismo de Estado: la doctrina de la seguridad nacional en el cono sur*, Caracas, Nueva Sociedad; México, DF, Editorial Nueva Imagen, 1980. Regarding political terrorism, we would like to highlight the work of Michel Wieviorka, *El terrorismo: la violencia política en el mundo*, epilogue to this edition by Mario Onaindía and Jorge M. Reverte, Spanish translation by Regina Martínez, Esplugues de Llobregat, Plaza y Janés, 1991. Grant Warlaw, *Terrorismo político: teoría, táctica y contramedidas*, Madrid, Estado Mayor del Ejército, 1986. Paul Wilkinson, *Terrorismo político*, Madrid, Felmar, 1976.

102 Regarding the topic of international law's answer to international terrorism, see Consuelo Ramón Chornet, *Terrorismo y respuesta de fuerza en el marco del Derecho internacional*, Valencia, Tirant Lo Blanch, 1993. Igor Bilischenko – Nikolai, Zhdanov, *El terrorismo como crimen internacional: (el terrorismo y el Derecho internacional)*, translated from Russian by M. Ciutat, Moscow, Progreso, 1983. Giuliana Ziccardi Capaldo, *Terrorismo internazionale e garanzie collective*, Milano, Giuffrè, 1990. See also, regarding the topic of international terrorism, Joss Irish, *Terrorismo internacional*, Barcelona, Producciones Editoriales, 1975. Jesús T. Cid Arambarría, *El terrorismo en el siglo XXI*, Madrid, Seguritecnia, 2002. Curso Internacional de Defensa (10.2002. Jaca), *Terrorismo internacional en el siglo XXI*, Madrid, Ministerio de Defensa, Secretaría General Técnica, 2003. Del Campo (*et al.*), directed by Salustiano Del Campo, *Terrorismo internacional*, Madrid, Instituto de Cuestiones Internacionales, 1984.

between civilian and political-military populations, or between the innocent and the guilty, and combines religious and ethnic aspects by answering a call to *holy war*. Together with this medieval inspiration (which reminds us of other religious wars fought in different contexts, like the Crusades), however, this new style of terrorism also employs modern methods (e.g. chemical, bacteriological and nuclear weapons, as well as pushing martyrs to commit suicide) which expand their destructive potential. What's more, international terrorism counts on important *economic support* from the huge fortunes of Arab magnates, especially from the Middle East, as well as on support from a large part of Islamic countries' populations and the complicity of some governments. All of this has converted such terrorism into a grave and asymmetric threat that is described well by the metaphor employed at the end of the 1980s by Ulrich Beck of a *society of risk*, which is unlike the kind of *perpetual peace* which prevailed during the Cold War, after World War II, in Western society.[103]

103 Regarding the topic is a very thought-provoking book by Bassam Bishuti, *Terrorismo: factor principal en la creación del "Estado de Israel"*, Madrid, Oficina de Información de la Liga de los Estados Árabes, 1973. Related to this topic, it can be affirmed that the Palestinian society is traumatized by its past which is synonymous with being uprooted and marked by five wars. There also exist challenges that obscure their future. Among them, of particular significance are: the de-territorialization of the Palestinian identity; the uncontrollable growth of the demographic; the emergence of a new generation of young Palestinians in occupied territories, fascinated by radical fundamentalist groups like the Jihad and Hamas; the future of the Christian communities, since many of their members are emigrating to new, calmer horizons, which leads to the possibility that perhaps one day there will no longer be Christians in the country that witnessed the birth of Christianity; the reactivation by the Palestinian Authority of the patronage system, in an environment with many large families and going against the aspirations of the Palestinian people for a democracy in which the social and political elite are cleared out; the problem of the refugees; the role of women in Palestinian society in resistance and diplomatic movements—such as Hanan Ashrawi or Leila Shahid, as well as many other discrete and anonymous figures. Regarding the subject, see Bichara Khader, "Los palestinos: un pueblo martirizado por la Historia," in Various Authors,, *La globalización y los derechos*

In all conflicts between two parties oftentimes both sides share, to some degree, a portion of the blame. And in the thunderstorm of controversy triggered by the inexcusable and unjustifiable 9/11 attacks, the media response to international terrorism, and the presence of the *perpetual war* in which we find ourselves, there is no shortage of voices that ask the uncomfortable, but unavoidable question: is the West in some way responsible for what is happening? Aren't the attacks nothing more than the logical consequence of an unjust situation that, according to some authors, has been perpetrated for centuries by the West due to its hegemonic domination over and exploitation of the poorest countries of the world, which have in turn been submitted to a kind of humiliation?[104] In short, isn't capitalism the major cause of all the world's evils? Can one speak of a war of civilizations? What level of truth is there in these questions?

To respond to this issue and not fall into the trap of simplification or demagogy, it is necessary to go back in time several years, to the situation immediately following the end of the Cold War and the disintegration of the Soviet Union.[105] At that time there was a proliferation of apparent states which were partially broken up and which served as the perfect breeding ground for the appearance and consolidation of mafia networks and different types of organized crime. Instead of authority, the ruling force in such groups was power. This power, which came through the force of weapons more than through the force of words, was in the hands of authentic private, well-armed armies that imposed their law on the weak in a kind of *bellum privata* in the purest Hobbesian tradition. In this war situation of everyone fighting against everyone else without a strong nation-state to keep things in check, individuals searched for

humanos. IV Jornadas Internacionales de Derechos Humanos (Sevilla, 2003), op. cit., pp. 45-60.

104 This is the topic of a book by T. Beláshenko (*et al.*), under the editing of Professor Y. Pankov, *El terrorismo político: inculpación al imperialismo*, translated from Russian by M. Kuznetsov, Moscú, Progreso, 1983.

105 Regarding this topic, see Ray S. Cline – Yonah Alexander, *Terrorismo: la conexión soviética*, Buenos Aires, Clio, 1984.

refuge in other types of entities, such as religion or ethnicity. Thus it can be affirmed that the postwar political order has ended. This reality is joined by the boom in political fundamentalism inspired by religious fundamentalism.[106]

5.3.2 Solutions to the Problem of Terrorism: Is There Room for a Utopia?

A The Value of Visionary Dreams

There is, however, no lack of those who are optimistic in the face of the problem of terrorism. They believe that terrorism can be defeated, as long as we attack the root causes of the problem. This is the perspective of Nicolás López Calera, when he affirms:

> *But I am of the belief that it is necessary to face up to the pessimism and disillusion, as much so in theory as in practice. It is necessary to face up to the conservative and decadent dogma that yells from the hillside that there is no alternative. It is necessary to fight for the utopian vision of a world without violence and, of course, without terrorist violence. Nothing is impossible. Perhaps it is necessary to specify that when it is said that something is impossible to do, what is really being said is that it has never been done before. If people act as though it is impossible to change things for the better, then it is guaranteed that there will not be changes for the better. (N. Chomsky)*[107]

I agree with the author about these thoughts. In fact, this book is based around the belief that ideas change the world. Not ideas by themselves. But ideas can help change things, when all other conditions are appropriate.

All of the extraordinary advances in history and humanity began with visions, dreams and utopias: nothing could be done with-

---

106 Ramón Vargas-Machuca Ortega, "Orden político y justicia frente al terrorismo global. A propósito del 11-S," in Pablo Badillo O'Farrell, Pluralismo, tolerancia, multiculturalismo…, op. cit., pp. 245-260.

107 Nicolás López Calera (ed.), *La palabra contra el terrorismo*, Granada, 2004. Especially the author's article, entitled "Terrorismo: luchar contra las causas," pp. 41-47; the quote is from p. 47.

out the will and capacity to imagine, to go beyond the experience of the pre-established order and to dream and take into consideration not only what *is*, but also what *could be.* Visions change the mental frameworks of humanity, allow age-old practices to be questioned, and permit progress. Historic visions were what allowed Galileo to discover that the Earth rotated around the sun and not the other way around; were what let Columbus discover America and see that our planet was not a flat disc, but rather a sphere; were what allowed the kings and emperors to stop considering themselves divine representatives; were what allowed the realization that social class divisions or castes were not something natural and were what allowed for the proclamation of the principle of equality for all human beings; visions were what led slavery and apartheid to be considered morally undesirable; were what let women have the same rights, at least formally, as men; or were what led torture and genocide to be condemned as disgusting practices.

Such visions bring out the best in us and are sources of inspiration that let us daydream. They are vehicles of hope for the future that elevate our spirit, even in times of great calamity. No great success has been achieved without a visionary mind that previously dreamed about it, that was able to rise above what for ages was considered *correct* and true, and that was able to challenge the established order.

But visions cannot become reality on their own. For this to happen they need people—men and women committed to action: political leaders; poets and philosophers that know how to inspire in others the belief in change; people capable of going beyond their own desires and of doing something altruistic in favor of everyone else; people willing to confront concealed powerful interests and do so with a fierce opposition that, sometimes posing a risk to their own lives, resists frustration and fear, and refuses to surrender to discouragement.[108]

108 As has been written by Aung San Suu Kyi, *Freedom from Fear*, New York, Penguin, 1995 ed., p. 183: "It is not enough to call on liberty, democracy, and human rights. There must exist the determination to persevere in the fight, to make sacrifices in the name of enduring truths, and to resist

B The Limit of Reality

There do need to be dreamers, but not naïve ones. One must not confuse dreams with reality—what *should be* with what *is*. Instead, one must keep their feet on the ground. Here is an example from daily life that illustrates this point.

If someone orders us to do something manifestly unacceptable—for instance, ordering us to jump out of a window—our answer will surely be to refuse the order, no matter how strong the links to authority, respect or power that this person exercises over our will. We would simply say something to the effect of: "*I'm sorry, I can't jump. If I did, I would probably kill myself, and I don't want to die.*"

Answers like the above, in other contexts, are preferred daily by thousands of human beings, without questioning the technical suitability or formal correctness of their answers. In reality, it is not accurate to say that we *cannot* jump out the window, unless we are literally physically impeded from doing so, by a paralysis or because we are tied up. On the actual level of being, or of the facts, nothing actually impedes us from jumping out the window. In fact, it would make more sense to say something along the lines of: "*I'm sorry, but as much as I value you, I should not obey you in this case, because it is not ethically right to end one's life, and if I jump out the window that is what I will be doing.*" Note here the change in approach. We have crossed the plane of what I *can* do to the plane of what I *should* do. Because *we should not do everything that we can do and, vice versa, we cannot do everything that we should do.* Now we are not situated on the actual level of the facts or of reality, but rather on the level of what should be and of values in accordance with certain ethical codes of morality, religion or natural law.

---

the corrupt temptations of desire, bad faith, ignorance and fear. It is said that the saints are just sinners that keep trying." Cited in Paul Gordon Lauren, "Nuevos retos de los derechos humanos. El futuro a la luz del pasado", *cit.*, p. 381. In this same line of proposing utopias, see the recent work of Nicolás López Calera, *¿Es posible un mundo justo? Estudios de Filosofía jurídica y política*, Granada, Universidad de Granada, 2003.

Why such an example? What I want to make clear with this example is that often these two levels are confused—the level of being and the level of what should be; facts and values. Also confused is the difference between an "explanation" (the causal description of causes and effects) and its "justification" (the value judgment in accordance with the notion of justice). This mix-up occurs in such a way that oftentimes what *cannot* be is confused with what *should* not be.

In the discourse surrounding terrorism, as is the case with many others, we should never mix dreams with reality or utopias with facts. At the same time, however, we should not forget that dreams serve to change the world because we have our feet too firmly planted on the ground. It is important, in this sense, to achieve the combination of realism and idealism, in that perfect middle ground where virtue lies—far from a sterile fantasy, but also from a paralyzing realism. It is necessary to dream, but without losing sight of reality. Oftentimes the discourse surrounding terrorism, confusing the level of being with the level of what should be, sins on the side of being excessively harsh or excessively unrealistic and, what is worse, is not conscious that it has fallen into the confusion of these levels.[109]

6 The Issue of "Gender"

One of the human groups that has suffered more discrimination than anyone else has been that of women. Up until not very many years ago, women were legally considered in our country as minors in ward. They were hindered from reaching well-paid or prestigious jobs in conditions of equality, and their function in life was limited almost exclusively to motherhood and taking care of the home. There are collectives of women, such as prostitutes or immigrants, whose rights are still diminished today and that can be considered as a case of social discrimination that should be fought. Another

109 The same idea of being a "realistic dreamer," but referring to the topic of punishment, is expressed in María José Falcón y Tella – Fernando Falcón y Tella, *Fundamento y finalidad de la sanción..., op. cit.*, pp. 247-251.

problem that affects this sector in a special way is that of violence and physical abuse against women. In the *Declaration on the elimination of violence against women*, of the General Assembly of the United Nations,[110] violence against women is defined as:

> *Physical, sexual and psychological violence occurring in the family, including battering, sexual abuse of female children in the household, dowry-related violence, marital rape, female genital mutilation and other traditional practices harmful to women; non-spousal violence and violence related to exploitation; physical, sexual and psychological violence occurring within the general community, including rape, sexual abuse, sexual harassment and intimidation at work, in educational institutions and elsewhere, trafficking in women and forced prostitution; physical, sexual and psychological violence perpetrated or condoned by the State, wherever it occurs.*

The recognition by the Hague Tribunal of the systematic violation of women as "crimes against humanity" came very late, in 1996. Also, precariousness regarding work and unemployment are quite feminized, considering the difficulties of obtaining attractive jobs (at least with a contract). These issues become even more of a problem among immigrants. Sexual activity is not a part of the job of the majority of immigrants, but the majority of sexual workers are immigrants.[111]

There are three possible models that can be applied to male-female relationships today: that of the "dependence" of the woman with respect to the man, that of complete "independence", and that of "interdependence" or joint responsibility.

The first model was present in Spain until its definitive abolition in the 1978 Constitution, although the normative framework that recognized this equality existed before, coming about with the reforms of the Civil Code in 1975. From this past perspective, the

110 (Res. A. G. 48/104, ONU, 1994).

111 Dolores Juliano, "Derechos Humanos y Género", in Various Authors, *La globalización y los derechos humanos. IV Jornadas Internacionales de Derechos Humanos (Sevilla, 2003), op. cit.*, pp. 18-26.

difference between the two sexes was exaggerated and the inferiority of women with respect to men was affirmed. It was thought that both sexes had different cultural roles and functions that were not interchangeable, and the social appraisal that men and women received was not the same. The man was assigned to act in the public sphere, guiding "production," while the woman was entrusted with the private realm, in relation to "reproduction." This model was surpassed a long time ago.

The second model emerges as a result of the demands of the first feminist movements in the 1960s, which understood the situation at the time as one of equality without any differences. Being the same for women meant inhabiting places in the public world that belonged to men. In other words, women wanted to "replace men," imitating masculine ways—an example of this is *unisex* fashion. Women flee from the private world, which they consider the cause of their slavery, to the corporate world, where they enter the job market. They attempted to make their voices heard and tried to reach formal equality in the legal realm. The presence of women in the public sphere is reflected in their abandonment and renunciation of the private world. Women had to pay liberation from motherhood as a price. It was also necessary to free themselves from men. As such, men turned into the enemy. Assimilationism was introduced, and considered that there was no difference between males and females, not even biologically. All social functions were considered interchangeable. It was affirmed that sexual differences were nonexistent. Equality was identified with homogeneity.

The third model advocates equality through the recognition of differences. This model demands that the two sexes must simultaneously be present in the private and public world. It demands a higher presence of females in public life and of males in domestic matters and child rearing. The model distinguishes between functions that are interchangeable in both realms—that can be accomplished indiscriminately by people of both sexes and only depend on learning—and functions or roles that are connected to biological differences and are not transferable between sexes.[112]

112 Regarding the impact of globalization on gender themes, see Dolors Renau (comp.); Micaela Navarro (*et al.*), *Globalización y mujer*, Madrid, Pablo Iglesias, 2002. Isel Ribero, "Globalización, desigualdad y mujer," in Micaela Navarro (*et al.*), Dolors Renau (coord.), *Globalización y mujer, op. cit.* Paloma de Villota (ed.), *Globalización y género*, prologue by José Luis Sampedro, Madrid, Síntesis, 1999. *Globalización a qué precio: el impacto en las mujeres del norte y del sur,* Barcelona, Icaria Antrazyt, 2001. Cecilia Castaño Collado, "Globalización y género," in Ramón Alós (*et al.*), *Sindicalismo y globalización*, Madrid, Confederación Sindical de Comisiones Obreras, 2002. Regarding the topic of affirmative action, specifically in German legislation and European law, see María Elósegui Itxaso, *Las acciones positivas para la igualdad de oportunidades laborales entre mujeres y hombres. Un análisis de la legislación alemana y la Directiva 76/207/CEE desde la teoría de la argumentación de Robert Alexy*, prologue by Juan José Gil Cremades, Madrid, Universidad de Zaragoza – Centro de Estudios Políticos y Constitucionales, 2003. Describing the three models cited above, see pp. 23-32. See also, in Italian, Letizia Gianformaggio (1944-2004), *Eguaglianza, donne e diritto.* A cura di Alessandra Facchi, Carla Faralli, Tamar Pitch, Bologna, Il Mulino, 2005.

III Some Concluding Thoughts

In these critical conclusions I do not want to just recapitulate the key ideas and points of views already expressed in the book, but rather I want to synthesize in a strong idea the core notions of the book and condense in a final claim the position that it takes. The book analyzes the challenges which are currently present in the field of human rights, such as: globalization, multiculturalism, universal criminal jurisdiction, the role of sovereignty, international terrorism, wars, and advances in biotechnology and the Internet. These subject matters are not isolated, and are in reality clearly interconnected. The meeting point, the driving force behind all of these topics, is the idea of acceleration and complexity that is linked to said phenomena in our time.

We live in the beginning of a new century and perhaps also in the beginning of a new era of human rights. In the last decades we have witnessed some advances which have been as original as they have been unexpected and rapid. These advances affirm that the categories of the past, a past which is not so distant, are no longer fit for the necessities of new realities. Old frameworks are not sufficient, and it is necessary to construct new explanatory models that can adapt to the three different worlds that divide reality: facts, rules and values, which together serve as another manifestation of the three-dimensional nature of things. Interdisciplinary approaches in this subject matter are necessary now more than ever. Life is so exceedingly complex that if we do not relate together the conclusions and knowledge reached in different branches of learning, and do so in the service of human rights, we run the risk of simplifying everything.

Currently, with the boom in new technologies, especially in the area of communications, any event can reach a global dimension. Globalization has resulted in great advancements. At this point moving backwards is not possible or desirable. But it is necessary to stop for a moment in this path of advancement to see what direction we want to go in. It is important to positively channel discoveries so that science does not devour man. After 9/11 nothing will be the same—this phrase has been repeated more than enough. International terrorism today forms a serious threat for the security of our world. But that does not justify defense at the cost of damaging fundamental freedoms, conquered by the rule of law. In this environment it is completely necessary for human rights to rise up as arbitrators in the world sphere in order to prevent any type of abuses.

Notable progress has been made, but there is still a long way to go. It is necessary to be vigilant and to avoid setbacks. Humanity has become the new subject of human rights. It is no longer an issue of the individual against the state, as was traditionally the case. All of society now has rights that can be enjoyed collectively, on a global scale. Peace, the defense of the environment, and so many other prospects are only feasible in today's world if governments, international organizations and civil society collaborate on a global scale.

We should not give in to discouragement. The fight for human rights continues. Learning from the lessons of the past, together we must contribute to constructing a fairer, better world for future generations. Between what "is" and what "should" or "could be," between dreams and reality, there is only one possible link: action. But, as the Irish playwright, critic and polemicist George Bernard Shaw said: "*He who can, does; he who cannot, teaches.*"[1] Whether it be from the political arena, the academic world or any other field in which someone's life unfolds, one must act and/or move others to action. I hope that the reflections expressed in this book contribute in some manner to that end or, if nothing else, hope that

1 The quote is in José Iturmendi Morales, "En torno a la '*Comunidad Sorda*' como comunidad de aprendizaje...", *cit.*, p. 10.

reading this work has not been an overly torturous experience for the reader.

IV Bibliography

ABELLÁN, Joaquín, "Los retos del multiculturalismo para el Estado moderno", in BADILLO O'FARRELL, Pablo (comp.), *Pluralismo, tolerancia, multiculturalismo..., op. cit.*, pp. 13-33.

ADDA, Jacques, *La globalización de la economía: orígenes y desafíos*, Spanish translation by Javier ORTEGA, with the cooperation of Fernando MINGUEZ and the final revision of the author, Madrid, Sequitur, 1999.

AGUELO NAVARRO, Pascual, "Derechos y libertades de los extranjeros", in *La globalización y los derechos humanos. IV Jornadas Internacionales de Derechos Humanos (Sevilla, 2003)*, Talasa Ediciones, pp. 90-102.

AGUIRRE, Mariano – FILESI, Teresa – GONZÁLEZ, Mabel, *Globalización y sistema internacional: Anuario CIP 2000*, Barcelona, Icaria (etc.), 2000.

AGUIRRE, Mariano (*et al.*), FLOR, José Ignacio (comp.), *Globalización, crisis ambiental y educación*, Madrid, Ministerio de Educación, Cultura y Deporte, Secretaría General Técnica, 2002.

ALÓS, Ramón – JÓDAR, Pere, "Globalización económica, cambios en los modelos de empresa, segmentación del trabajo y relaciones laborales", in Ramón ALÓS (*et al.*), *Sindicalismo y globalización*, Madrid, Confederación Sindical de Comisiones Obreras, 2002.

ÁLVAREZ DORREGO, Matías, *La Corte Penal Internacional: hacia la inclusión en el Estatuto de Roma del crimen de terrorismo*, Buenos Aires, Fabián J. de Plácido, 2004.

ÁLVAREZ MERAYO, José Antonio - FERNÁNDEZ FERNÁNDEZ, Maximiliano – BENA BUA, Pilar (comps.), *La globalización y sus efectos en los inicios del tercer milenio: actas del ciclo organizado por la Universidad Católica de Ávila, Ávila, 15 de febrero a 5 de abril de 2001*, Ávila, Universidad Católica de Ávila, 2001.

AMIN, Samir – HOUTART, François (eds.), *Globalización de las resistencias: el estado de las luchas* (from the original: *Mondialisation des résistances: l'état des luttes*), Barcelona, Icaria; Madrid, Cáritas Española, 2003.

ANDRÉS SÁENZ DE SANTA MARÍA, María Paz, "Sanciones internacionales (Derecho Internacional Público)", in *Enciclopedia Jurídica Básica*, t. IV, Madrid, Civitas, 1995, pp. 6063-6065.

AÑÓN ROIG, María José (*et al.*), *La universalidad de los derechos sociales: el reto de la inmigración*, Valencia, Universidad de Valencia, Servicio de Publicaciones, 1rst ed., 1rst reprint, 2004.

ARA PINILLA, Ignacio, *Las transformaciones de los derechos humanos*, Madrid, Tecnos, 1990.

ARELLANO, Fernando (*et al.*) (eds.), Varinia ROMÁN (comp.), *Globalización, Seattle y estrategias ciudadanas*, Santiago de Chile, LOM, 2000.

BADILLO O'FARRELL, Pablo (comp.), *Pluralismo, tolerancia, multiculturalismo. Reflexiones para un mundo plural*, Madrid, AKAL-Universidad Internacional de Andalucía, 2003.

- "¿Pluralismo versus multiculturalismo?", in BADILLO O'FARRELL, Pablo (comp.), *Pluralismo, tolerancia, multiculturalismo..., op. cit.*, pp. 33-67.

BARAÑANA CID, Margarita, *La globalización económica: incidencia en las relaciones sociales y económicas*, Madrid, Consejo General del Poder Judicial, 2002.

BAREA, Maite – BILLÓN, Margarita, *Globalización y nueva economía*, Madrid, Encuentro, 2002.

BARRACA MAIRAL, Javier (*et al.*); ROA, Francisco J. (comp.), *Globalización, Internet y marketing: una respuesta ética*, Murcia, Universidad Católica San Antonio, 2003.

BAUMAN, Gerd, *El enigma multicultural*, Barcelona, Paidós, 2001.

BAUMAN, Zygmunt, *La globalización: consecuencias humanas*, Spanish translation by Daniel ZADUNAISKY, México (etc.), Fondo de

Cultura Económica, 1999. 2nd Spanish ed., 2001; 2nd Spanish ed., 1rst reprint. 2003.

BEAUMONT, Gustav de – TOCQUEVILLE, Alexis de, *On the Penitentiary System in the United States*, Philadelphia, 1833.

BELÁSHENKO, T. (*et al.*), written by Professor Y. PANKOV, *El terrorismo político: inculpación al imperialismo*, Spanish translation M. KUZNETSOV, Moscú, Progreso, 1983.

BERGER, Peter L. – HUNTINGTON, Samuel P., *Globalizaciones múltiples: la diversidad cultural en el mundo contemporáneo*, Barcelona, Paidós, 2002.

BERNALDO DE QUIRÓS (*et al.*), *La globalización*, Madrid, Fundación para el Análisis y los Estudios Sociales, D. L., 2002.

BESTARD COMAS, Joan, *Globalización, tercer mundo y solidaridad: estudio comparativo entre los Informes del Programa de las Naciones Unidas para el Desarrollo (PNUD) y los documentos de la Doctrina Social de la Iglesia (DSI)*, Madrid, Biblioteca de Autores Cristianos, 2003.

BIFANI, Paolo, *La globalización: ¿otra caja de Pandora?*, Granada, Universidad de Granada, 2002.

BILISCHENKO, Igor – ZHDANOV, Nikolai, *El terrorismo como crimen internacional: (el terrorismo y el Derecho internacional)*, Spanish translation by M. CIUTAT, Moscow, Progreso, 1983.

BISHUTI, Bassam, *Terrorismo: factor principal en la creación del "Estado de Israel"*, Madrid, Oficina de Información de la Liga de los Estados Árabes, 1973.

BOCARDO CRESPO, Enrique, "Los asaltos al pluralismo", in BADILLO O'FARRELL, Pablo (comp.), *Pluralismo, tolerancia, multiculturalismo…*, *op. cit.*, pp. 67-107.

BONANNO, Alessandro (comp.), *Globalización del sector agrícola y alimentario*, Madrid, Ministerio de Agricultura, Pesca y Alimentación, 1994.

BORDES SOLANAS, Montserrat, *El terrorismo: una lectura analítica*, Barcelona, Ediciones Bellaterra, 2000.

BORDO, Michael D. – PANINI MURSHID, Antu, *Globalization and Changing Patterns in the International Transmision of Stocks in*

Financial Markets, Cambridge –Massachusetts-, National Bureau of Economic Research, 2002.

BRÜNNER, Joaquín, *Globalización cultural y posmodernidad*, Santiago de Chile (...), Fondo de Cultura Económica, 1rst ed., 2nd reprint, 2002.

CABEZUDO RODRÍGUEZ, Nicolás, *La Corte Penal Internacional*, Madrid, Dykinson, 2002.

CALDERÓN, Fernando (comp.), *¿Es sostenible la globalización en América Latina?: debates con Manuel Castells, vol. 1, La globalización y América Latina*, Santiago de Chile, Fondo de Cultura Económica, 2003.

CALVO CARAVACA, Alfonso Luis – BLANCO-MORALES LIMONES, Pilar (eds.), *Globalización y Derecho*, Madrid, Colex, 2003.

CAMPAGNA, María Cristina – MASON, Alfredo, *Teoría del Estado. Cuando la filosofía y la política construyen la realidad.* Buenos Aires. Editorial Biblos. 1997.

CARRILLO SALCEDO, Juan Antonio, *Globalización y orden internacional: lección inaugural leída en la solemne apertura del Curso Académico 2004-2005 en la Universidad de Sevilla*, Sevilla, Universidad, 2004.

CARRIQUIRY, Guzmán (1944-), *Globalización e identidad católica en América Latina*, preface by Norberto Cardenal RIVERA CARRERA, México, D.F., Barcelona, Plaza & Janés, 2002.

CASADO GONZÁLEZ, María, *Bioética, Derecho y Sociedad*, Madrid, Trotta, 1998.

CASALS, Carles, *Globalización: apuntes de un proceso que está transformando nuestras vidas*, Barcelona, Interpón, 2001.

CASTAÑO COLLADO, Cecilia, "Globalización y género", in Ramón ALÓS (*et al.*), *Sindicalismo y globalización*, Madrid, Confederación Sindical de Comisiones Obreras, 2002.

CASTRO TOLEDO, Beatriz, "Consideraciones sobre la licitud e ilicitud de la tortura", in Various Authors, *El concepto de relevancia jurídica (Estudios de la Sección de Filosofía del Derecho. Real Academia de Jurisprudencia y Legislación)*, Madrid, Centro de Estudios Registrales, 2001, pp. 249-263.

CÉSAR DACHARY, Alfredo – ARNAIZ BURNE, Stella Maris, *Globalización, turismo y sustentabilidad,* Guadalajara (México), Universidad de Guadalajara. Centro Universitario de la Costa, Campus Puerto Vallarta, 2002.

CID ARAMBARRÍA, Jesús T., *El terrorismo en el siglo XXI,* Madrid, Seguritecnia, 2002.

CLINE, Ray S. – ALEXANDER, Yonah, *Terrorismo: la conexión soviética,* Buenos Aires, Clio, 1984.

COLLON, Michel, *La guerra global ha comenzado.* CHOMSKY, Noam, *La nueva guerra contra el terror.* PETRAS, James, *Los intelectuales y la guerra: de la retirada a la rendición.* CASTRO, Fidel (1926-), *El terrorismo, la guerra y la crisis económica,* Hondarribia, Guipúzcoa, Hiru, 3rd ed., 2002.

COMAS D'ARGEMIR, Dolors, "La globalización, ¿unidad del sistema?: exclusión social, diversidad y diferencia cultural en la aldea global", in Noam CHOMSKY (*et al.*), *Los límites de la globalización,* Barcelona, Ariel, 2002.

COMBACAU, J., *Le pouvoir de sanctions de l'ONU (Étude théorique de la coercition militaire),* Paris, 1974.

COMISIÓN EUROPEA, DIRECCIÓN GENERAL DE PRENSA Y COMUNICACIÓN, *La globalización en beneficio de todos: la Unión Europea y el comercio mundial,* Luxemburgo, Oficina de Publicaciones Oficiales de las Comunidades Europeas, 2003.

CONGRESO IREC 2001, *Conferencia sobre relaciones laborales en Europa (2001, Madrid), Globalización, competitividad y gobierno del empleo y de las condiciones de empleo en Europa: estructuras, actores y estrategias: estado de la cuestión. Organizada por la Escuela de Relaciones Laborales de la Universidad Complutense de Madrid, con la colaboración de la Facultad de Ciencias Políticas y Sociología de la UCM,* Madrid, s. n., 2001.

CONGRESO REGIONAL AMERICANO DE DERECHO DEL TRABAJO Y DE LA SEGURIDAD SOCIAL (4. 1998. SANTIAGO DE CHILE), *Globalización económica y derecho individual del trabajo,* Santiago de Chile, Sociedad Internacional de Derecho del Trabajo y de la Seguridad Social, 1998.

CRESPO NAVARRO, Elena, *Nuevas formas de protección del individuo en Derecho internacional. La erosión del vínculo de la nacionalidad,* Valencia, Tirant Lo Blanch, 2005.

CUADRADO GAMARRA, Nuria, *Aplicación de los sistemas expertos al campo del Derecho,* Preface by Emilio SUÑÉ LLINÁS, Servicio de Publicaciones, Facultad de Derecho, Universidad Complutense de Madrid, 2004.

CURSO INTERNACIONAL DE DEFENSA (10.2002. Jaca), *Terrorismo internacional en el siglo XXI,* Madrid, Ministerio de Defensa, Secretaría General Técnica, 2003.

CHOSSUDOVSKY, Michel, *Globalización de la pobreza y nuevo orden mundial,* 1rst Spanish ed., Buenos Aires, Siglo Veintiuno, 2002.

DAVID, Pedro R., *Globalización, prevención del delito y justicia penal,* Buenos Aires, Zavalia, 1999.

DAVIDSON, Alastair –WEEKLEY, Kathleen, *Globalization and Citizenship in the Asia-Pacific,* New York, St. Martin's Press, 1999.

DEHESA, Guillermo de la, *Globalización, desigualdad y pobreza,* Madrid, Alianza, 2003.

DEL CAMPO (*et al.*), directed by Salustiano DEL CAMPO, *Terrorismo internacional,* Madrid, Instituto de Cuestiones Internacionales, 1984.

DEL VECCHIO, Angela, *Giurisdizione internazionale e globalizzazione. I tribunali internazionali tra globalizzazione e frammentazione,* Milano, Giuffrè, 2003.

DELLA PORTA, Donatella (1956-), *Il terrorismo di sinistra,* Bologna, Il Mulino, 1990.

DÍAZ, Carlos (*et al.*), *Globalización y persona,* Madrid, Unión Editorial, 2003.

DÍAZ MIER, Miguel Ángel (ed.), *La globalización: un estudio interdisciplinario,* Alcalá, Universidad de Alcalá, Instituto Universitario de Investigación de Estudios Norteamericanos, 2004.

DOMÍNGUEZ, Carlos Horacio, *El terrorismo en el Estado de Derecho,* preface by Osiris G. VILLEGAS, Buenos Aires, Abaco de Rodolfo Depalma, 1983.

DONOSO, Vicente, "Globalización: una perspectiva Norte/Sur", in Ramón ALÓS (*et al.*), *Sindicalismo y globalización*, Madrid, Confederación Sindical de Comisiones Obreras, 2002.

DUGUIT, Léon (1859-1928), *Le trasformazioni dello Stato: antologia di scritti*. A cura di Augusto BARBERA, Carla FARALLI, Massimiliano PANARARI, Torino, G. Giappichelli, 2003.

DWORKIN, Ronald (*et al.*) (eds.), *The Legacy of Isaiah Berlin*, New York, New York Review Books, 2001.

DWORKIN, Ronald, *Taking Rights Seriously*, London, Duckworth & Co. Ltd., 3rd ed, 1981; there is a Spanish translation by Marta GUASTAVINO, *Los derechos en serio*, Barcelona, Ariel, 1984. Barcelona, Planeta-Agostini, 1992.

- *Ética privada e igualitarismo político*, Spanish translation by Antoni DOMÈNECH, Barcelona, Paidós, 1993.

- "Do Liberal Values Conflict?", in DWORKIN, Ronald (*et al.*) (eds.), *The Legacy..., op. cit.*, pp. 73-90.

EICHENGREEN, Barry, *La globalización del capital: historia del sistema monetario internacional*, Spanish translation by María Esther RABASCO, Barcelona, Bosch, 2000.

ELBAZ, Mikhaël - HELLY, Dense (dirs.), *Globalización, ciudadanía y multiculturalismo*, preface to the Spanish edition by Enrique E. RAYA LOZANO, Granada, Maristán, 2002.

ELÓSEGUI ITXASO, María, *Las acciones positivas para la igualdad de oportunidades laborales entre mujeres y hombres. Un análisis de la legislación alemana y la Directiva 76/207/CEE desde la teoría de la argumentación de Robert Alexy*, Preface by Juan José Gil Cremades, Madrid, Universidad de Zaragoza – Centro de Estudios Políticos y Constitucionales, 2003.

EL TRIBUNAL PENAL INTERNACIONAL, Barcelona, Revista del Centre d'Estudis Juridics i Formació Espècializtzada, Forum, 2, 2003.

EL TRIBUNAL PENAL INTERNACIONAL: MESA REDONDA ORGANIZADA POR LA ASOCIACIÓN DE EX DIPUTADOS Y EX SENADORES DE LAS CORTES GENERALES DE ESPAÑA, CELEBRADA EN MADRID EL 28 DE JUNIO DE 1999, Madrid, Cortes Generales, 2000.

ESCOBAR GUERRERO, Miguel, *Globalización y utopía*, México, UNAM, 2001.

ESCUDERO ESPINOSA, Juan Francisco, *La Corte Penal Internacional y el Consejo de Seguridad: hacia una paz por la justicia*, Madrid, Editorial Diles, 2004.

ESTAY, Jaime – GIRÓN, Alicia – MARTÍNEZ, Osvaldo (comps.), *La globalización de la economía mundial: principales dimensiones en el umbral del siglo XXI*, México, Universidad Nacional Autónoma de México, Instituto de Investigaciones Económicas, 1999.

ESTÉBANEZ ÁLVAREZ, José, *Globalización, espacio y geografía*, León, 1995.

FALCÓN Y TELLA, Fernando, *Tridimensionalismo y Derecho*, Madrid, Servicio de Publicaciones, Facultad de Derecho, Universidad Complutense de Madrid, 2004. Reviewed by Juan Antonio MARTÍNEZ MUÑOZ, in *Foro, Revista de Ciencias Jurídicas y Sociales, Facultad de Derecho, Universidad Complutense de Madrid*, 0/2004, pp. 317-320.

- "Valeurs, Norms et Faits dans le Droit", in *Revue Interdisciplinaire d'Études Juridiques*, 53, December 2004, pp. 123-139.

FALCÓN Y TELLA, María José, *La desobediencia civil*, preface by Fernando GARRIDO FALLA, Madrid, Marcial Pons, 2000. Reviews by: Guido SARACENI, in *Rivista Internazionale di Filosofia del Diritto*, 3, 2001, pp. 424-426; Paula LÓPEZ ZAMORA, in *Revista de Estudios Políticos*, 111, pp. 312-314; Beatriz CASTRO TOLEDO, in *Revista de la Facultad de Derecho de la Universidad Complutense de Madrid*, 2001, pp. 241-263; Oscar Mª PRIETO GARCÍA, in *Anuario de Derechos Humanos, Nueva Época*, vol. 2, Instituto de Derechos Humanos, Facultad de Derecho, Universidad Complutense de Madrid, 2001, pp. 1026-1035; Juan Antonio MARTÍNEZ MUÑOZ, in *Siglo Veintiuno, Revista de Pensamiento y Cultura*, 53, Spring 2002, pp. 146-148; and Pedro RIVAS, "De nuevo sobre la desobediencia civil", in *Anales de la Cátedra Francisco Suárez*, 34, 2000, pp. 447-450. There is an English translation by Peter MUCKLEY, First Part: *Civil Disobedience*, preface by Martti KOSKENNIEMI, Boston-Leiden, Martinus Nijhoff Publishers, 2004; Second part: *A History of Civil Disobedience*, Genève, Editions Diversités, 2004.

- "Las generaciones de derechos y la guerra", in *Anuario de Derechos Humanos, Nueva Época*, vol. 4, 2003, Instituto de Derechos Humanos, Facultad de Derecho, Universidad Complutense de Madrid, pp. 35-55.

- *El ciudadano frente a la ley*, Buenos Aires-Madrid, Editorial Ciudad Argentina-Universidad Complutense de Madrid, 2004. 2nd ed. 2006

FALCÓN Y TELLA, María José – FALCÓN Y TELLA, Fernando, *Fundamento y finalidad de la sanción: ¿un derecho a castigar?*, Preface by Antonio GARCÍA-PABLOS, Madrid, Marcial Pons, 2005. Reviews by: María Eugenia PÉREZ MONTERO, in *Anuario de Derechos Humanos, Nueva Época*, vol. 6, Instituto de Derechos Humanos, Facultad de Derecho, Universidad Complutense de Madrid, 2005, pp. 790-798; Ana VALERO FERNÁNDEZ DE PALENCIA, in *Foro. Revista de Ciencias Jurídicas y Sociales, Facultad de Derecho, Universidad Complutense de Madrid*, 2, 2005; and José María CARABANTE MUNTADA, in *ARSP* (forhcoming); there is an English translation, *Punishment and Culture: A Right to Punish?*, by Peter MUCKLEY, Boston-Leiden, Martinus Nijhoff Publishers, 2006.

FALK, Richard, *La globalización depredadora: una crítica*, Spanish translation by Herminia BEVIA y Antonio RESINES, Madrid, Siglo Veintiuno de España, 2002.

FARALLI, Carla, *Diritto e magia: il realismo di Hägerström e il positivismo filosofico*, Bologna, Clueb, 1987.

- *John Dewey: una filosofia del diritto per la democrazia*, 2nd ed., Bologna, Clueb, 1990.

- *La filosofia del diritto contemporanea. I temi e le sfide*, Roma, Laterza, 2002. 5rst ed. Threre is Spanish translation by María José FALCÓN Y TELLA and Juan Antonio MARTÍNEZ MUÑOZ, adapted to the spanish legal system and with notes by José ITURMENDI MORALES, Argentina-Madrid, Editorial Ciudad Argentina-Universidad Complutense de Madrid, 2007.

FARALLI, Carla – FERRARI, Vincenzo (eds.), *Laws and Rights: Proceedings of the International Congress of Sociology of Law for the Ninth Cent. of the University of Bologna: May 30-June 3, 1988: 2. Working Groups*, Milano, Giuffrè, 1993.

FARALLI, Carla – PATTARO, Enrico (curatori), *Reason in Law: Proceedings of the Conference Held in Bologna, 12-15 December 1986*, Milano, Giuffrè, 1987.

FARIÑAS DULCE, María José, *Globalización, ciudadanía y derechos humanos*, "Cuadernos Bartolomé de las Casas", 16, Madrid, Dykinson, 2000.

FARRÉ, Mariona – ALLEPUZ, Rafael (eds.), *Globalización y dependencia: efectos de la mundialización sobre el desarrollo de los pueblos*, Lleida, Edicions de la Universitat de Lleida, 2001.

FERLICCA, Roberto, *Terrorismo ácido*, Milano, Greco & Greco, 1991.

FERNÁNDEZ, Arturo – GAVEGLIO, Silvia (comps.), *Globalización, integración, Mercosur y desarrollo local*, Rosario, Homo Sapiens, 2000.

FERNÁNDEZ DURÁN, Ramón – ETXEZARRETA, Miren – SÁEZ BAYONA, Manolo, *Globalización capitalista: luchas y resistencias*, Barcelona, Virus, 2001.

FILOSOFI DEL DIRITTO CONTEMPORANI. A cura di Gianfrancesco ZANETTI; introduction by Carla FARALLI, Milano, R. Cortina, 1999.

FONTANA I LAZARO, Josep, *La globalización en una perspectiva histórica*, Oviedo, Universidad de Oviedo, 2003.

FORO "IGNACIO ELLACURÍA" SOLIDARIDAD Y CRISTIANISMO, *Conferencias sobre La globalización y sus excluidos*, Estella (Navarra), Verbo Divino, 1999. 3rd ed., 2002.

FROSINI, Vittorio, *L'uomo artificiale. Etica e diritto nell'era planetaria*, Milano, Spirali, 1986.

-*Law and Liberty in the Computer Age*, Oslo, Tano, 1995.

-*La democrazia nel XXI secolo*, Roma, Ideazione, 1997.

GAGO GUERRERO, Pedro, "El Estado social como obstáculo para el bienestar social", in *Cuadernos de Trabajo Social*, 3, 1990, pp. 57-67.

GALEOTTI, Anna Elisabetta, *Multiculturalismo. Filosofia politica e conflitto identitario*, Napoli, Liguori, 1999.

GAMBINA, Julio (comp.), *La globalización económico-financiera: su impacto en América Latina*, Buenos Aires, CLACSO, 2002.

GARCÍA-BERRIO, Teresa, *Informática y libertades. La protección de datos personales y su regulación en Francia y España,* Murcia, Servicio de Publicaciones de la Universidad de Murcia, 2003.

GARCÍA CANCLINI, Néstor, *La globalización imaginada,* Buenos Aires, Paidós, Colección "Paidós Estado y Sociedad", 1999.

GARCÍA DÍAZ, Miguel Ángel, "Globalización en positivo", in Ramón ALÓS (*et al.*), *Sindicalismo y globalización,* Madrid, Confederación Sindical de Comisiones Obreras, 2002.

GARCÍA ECHEVARRÍA, Santiago, *Globalización de la economía y dinámica de cambio de la empresa comercial: hacia una nueva cultura empresarial,* Alcalá de Henares, Universidad de Alcalá, Instituto de Dirección y Organización de Empresa, 1995.

GARCÍA GUITIÁN, Elena, "La repercusión política del pluralismo valorativo", in BADILLO O'FARRELL, Pablo (comp.), *Pluralismo, tolerancia, multiculturalismo..., op. cit.*, pp. 107-125.

GARCÍA MORALES, Aniza Fernanda, *La justiciabilidad de los derechos económicos, sociales y culturales (desc),* Instituto de Derechos Humanos, Madrid, Servicio de Publicaciones, Facultad de Derecho, Universidad Complutense de Madrid, 2003.

GARCÍA RAMÍREZ, Sergio, *La Corte Penal Internacional,* México, Instituto Nacional de Ciencias Penales, 2002.

GARCÍA SAN PEDRO, José, *Terrorismo: aspectos criminológicos y legales,* Madrid, Universidad Complutense, Facultad de Derecho – Ministerio de Justicia. Centro de Estudios Jurídicos, 1993.

GARRIGA DOMÍNGUEZ, A., *La protección de los datos personales en el Derecho español,* preface by Antonio-Enrique PÉREZ LUÑO, Madrid, Universidad Carlos III & Dykinson, 1999.

- *Tratamiento de datos personales y derechos fundamentales,* Madrid, Dykinson, 2004.

GARZÓN VALDÉS, Ernesto, "Optimismo y pesimismo en la democracia", in *Claves de Razón Práctica,* 131, 2003.

GEORGE, Susan – WOLF, Martin, *La globalización liberal: a favor y en contra,* Spanish translation by Jaime ZULAIKA, Barcelona, Anagrama, 2002.

GEORGE, Susan (*et al.*), edited by Matthew J. GIBNEY, *La globalización de los derechos humanos*, from the English original *Globalizing Rights*, Barcelona, Crítica, 2004.

GIANFORMAGGIO, Letizia (1944-2004), *Eguaglianza, donne e diritto*. A cura di Alessandra FACCHI, Carla FARALLI, Tamar PITCH, Bologna, Il Mulino, 2005.

GILBERT, Paul, *Terrorismo, nacionalismo, pacificación*, foreword by Manuel GARRIDO, Spanish translation by Marco Aurelio GALMATINI, Madrid, Ediciones Cátedra, 1998.

GINER, Salvador (*et al.*); REINARES-NESTARES, Fernando (comp.), *Terrorismo y sociedad democrática*, Madrid, Akal, 1982.

GLOBALIZACIÓN, CRECIMIENTO Y PROBREZA: CONSTRUYENDO UNA ECONOMÍA MUNDIAL INCLUYENTE, Washington, Banco Mundial; Bogotá, Alfaomega, Cop. 2002.

GLOBALIZACIÓN, MIGRACIONES Y DESARROLLO: INFORME DEL MILENIO, PROPUESTAS CLAVES PARA EL MILENIO, DECLARACIÓN DEL MILENIO, Madrid, Movimiento Contra la Intolerancia, 2001?

GLOBALIZACIÓN Y EDUCACIÓN, Pamplona, Universidad de Navarra, 2001.

GÓMEZ COLOMER, Juan-Luis, *El Tribunal Penal Internacional: investigación y acusación: (un estudio comparado sobre la influencia de modelos y realidades en el tratamiento del principio acusatorio en las fases previas al juicio del proceso penal ante el Tribunal Penal Internacional*, Valencia, Tirant Lo Blanch, 2003.

GONZÁLEZ CALLEJA, Eduardo, *El terrorismo en Europa*, Madrid, Arco Libros, 2002.

GONZÁLEZ JIMÉNEZ, Manuel, "El problema de la tolerancia en la España de las tres culturas", in BADILLO O'FARRELL (comp.), *Pluralismo, tolerancia, multiculturalismo…*, *op. cit.*, pp. 125-143.

GONZÁLEZ MÁRQUEZ, Felipe, "Globalización del terror", in RASHID, Ahmed (*et al.*), *El mundo después del 11 de septiembre de 2001*, Barcelona, Península, 2002, pp. 47-51.

GOWLLAND-DEBBAS, V., *Collective Responses to Illegal Acts in International Law*, Dordrecht, 1990.

GUERRA-BORGES, Alfredo, *Globalización e integración latinoamericana*, México, Siglo XXI, 2002.

GUILLOCHON, Bernard, *La globalización: ¿un futuro para todos?*, Barcelona, Spes, 2003.

HABERMAS, Jürgen, *El futuro de la naturaleza humana. ¿Hacia una eugenesia liberal?*, Spanish translation by R. S. CARBÓ, Barcelona, Paidós, 2002; review by María Eugenia PÉREZ MONTERO, in *Anuario de Derechos Humanos, Nueva Época*, Instituto de Derechos Humanos, Facultad de Derecho, Universidad Complutense de Madrid, vol. 4, 2003, pp. 437-444.

- *El Occidente escindido*, Madrid, Trotta, 2006.

HELD, David (1951-) – McGREW, Anthony , *Globalización – Antiglobalización: sobre la reconstrucción del orden mundial*, Spanish translation by Andrés DE FRANCISCO, Barcelona (etc.), Paidós, 2003.

HERRERA GARCÍA, Beatriz, *Globalización y sistema financiero*, Lima, Fondo Editorial Universidad Nacional Mayor de San Marcos, 2003.

IRANZO MARTÍN, Juan E., *Globalización y nueva economía*, Madrid, Instituto de Estudios Económicos, 2003.

IRISH, Joss, *Terrorismo internacional*, Barcelona, Producciones Editoriales, 1975.

ITURMENDI MORALES, José, "Acerca de la Historia recordada", in Various Authors, *Manuel Fraga. Homenaje Académico*. I, Madrid, Fundación Cánovas del Castillo, 1997, pp. 789-853

- "Proceso y muerte de Sócrates. Un sabio ante la justicia de su tiempo", in *Grandes abogados, grandes procesos que hicieron historia*, Pamplona, Aranzadi, 1997, pp. 155-159.

- "Hacia un nuevo Derecho internacional", in *Algunas cuestiones clave para el siglo XXI*, Colección Veintiuno, Madrid, Fundación Cánovas del Castillo, 2000, pp. 99-125.

- "¿Hacia un nuevo Derecho internacional?", in *Anuario de Derechos Humanos, Nueva Época*, vol. 2, Instituto de Derechos Humanos, Facultad de Derecho, Universidad Complutense de Madrid, 2001, pp. 523-779.

- "Derecho, Sanidad y derecho a la protección de la salud en un contexto social, cultural, económico y tecnológico en transformación", in Eduardo MARTÍNEZ Y HERNÁNDEZ – Luis Francisco GARCÍA PERULLES – Enrique BARÓN CRESPO, *Tratado del derecho a la protección de la salud*, Madrid, Servicio de Publicaciones, Facultad de Derecho, Universidad Complutense de Madrid, 2004, pp. 345-687.

- "En torno a la "*Comunidad Sorda*" como comunidad de aprendizaje y de prácticas de pertenencia y de fidelidad. Una aportación al debate entre comunitaristas y liberales acerca de los derechos, los valores y la Sociedad", in various authors, José Gabriel STORCH DE GRACIA Y ASENSIO (coord.), *Estatuto jurídico de las lenguas de señas en el Derecho español. Aproximaciones*, Madrid, Editorial Universitaria Ramón Areces, 2005, Lesson 1, pp. 3-227.

JALFEN, Luis Jorge (1940-), *Globalización y lógica virtual*, Buenos Aires, Argentina, Corregidor, 1998.

JOPPKE, Christian – LUKES, Steven (eds.), *Multicultural Questions*, Oxford, Oxford University Press, 1999.

JUERGENSMEYER, Mark, *Terrorismo religioso: el auge global de la violencia religiosa*, Madrid, Siglo XXI, 2001.

JULIANO, Dolores, "Derechos Humanos y Género", in various authors, *La globalización y los derechos humanos. IV Jornadas Internacionales de Derechos Humanos (Sevilla, 2003), op. cit.*, pp. 18-26.

JULIOS-CAMPUZANO, Alfonso de, *La globalización ilustrada: ciudadanía, derechos humanos y constitucionalismo*, "Cuadernos Bartolomé de las Casas", Madrid, Dykinson, 2003.

KABUNDA, Mbuyi, "Globalización y derechos humanos en África", in Various Authors, *La globalización y los derechos humanos, IV Jornadas Internacionales de Derechos Humanos (Sevilla, 2003),* Talasa Ediciones, op. cit., pp. 60-90.

KEKES, John, *The Morality of Pluralism*, Princeton, NJ, Princeton University Press, 1993.

KELSEN, Hans, "Absolutismo y relativismo en Filosofía y en Política", in *Qué es Justicia*. pp. 113-125.

KHADER, Bichara, "Los palestinos: un pueblo martirizado por la Historia", in Various Authors, *La globalización y los derechos humanos. IV Jornadas Internacionales de Derechos Humanos (Sevilla, 2003), op. cit.*, pp. 45-60.

KHOR, Martin, *La globalización desde el sur: estrategias para el siglo XXI*, Spanish translation by Clio BUGEL, from *Globalization and the South*, Barcelona, Icaria, 2001.

KOLODKO, Grzegorz W., *Globalización y perspectivas de desarrollo en los antiguos países comunistas*, Madrid, Siddhart Mehta, 2003.

KOSKENNIEMI, Martti, *El discreto civilizador de naciones. El auge y caída del Derecho internacional 1870-1960*, Spanish translation by Natalia ZARAGOZÁ GARCÍA, revision by Paula ALBERRO and Fernando FALCÓN Y TELLA, from the 1rst English edition -*The Gentle Civilizer of Nations. The Rise and Fall of International Law 1870-1960*, Cambridge, Cambridge University Press, 2001-, Buenos Aires-Madrid, Ciudad Argentina-Servicio de Publicaciones de la Facultad de Derecho de la Universidad Complutense de Madrid, 2005.

KRUGMAN, Paul R., *La globalización de la economía y las crisis financieras: lecciones de economía*, La Coruña, Instituto de Estudios Económicos de Galicia Pedro Barrié de la Maza, 1999.

KUPPERMAN, Robert H. (1935-) –TRENT, Darrell M., *Terrorismo: minaccia, realtá, difesa*, preface by Walter LAQUEAR, Roma, Bulzoni, 1981.

KYMLICKA, Will (ed.), *The Rights of Minority Cultures*, Oxford, Oxford University Press, 1995.

- *Ciudadanía multicultural. Una teoría liberal de los derechos de las minorías*, Barcelona-Buenos Aires-México, Paidós, 1996.

- *Finding Our Way. Rethinking Ethnocultural Relations in Canada*, Toronto-New York, Oxford University Press, 1998.

KYMLICKA, Will – HE, Baogang, *Multuculturalism in Asia*, Oxford-New York, Oxford University Press, 2005.

LAGARES, D., *Internet y el Derecho*, Barcelona, Ediciones Carena, 2nd ed., 2000.

LA GLOBALIZACIÓN Y LOS DERECHOS HUMANOS, *IV Jornadas Internacionales de Derechos Humanos (Sevilla, 2003)*, Madrid, Talasa Ediciones, 2004.

LAQUEUR, Walter (1921-), *Terrorismo*, Spanish translation by José Luis LÓPEZ MUÑOZ, Madrid, Espasa-Calpe, 1980.

LAUREN, Paul Gordon, "Nuevos retos para los derechos humanos. El futuro a la luz del pasado", conference given in the II Jornadas Internacionales "Nuevos retos de los derechos humanos", held by the Instituto de Derechos Humanos, in November 2003, in the Facultad de Derecho of the Universidad Complutense de Madrid. Spanish translation from the English original: "New Challenges for Human Rights: The Future in Light of the Past", by Fernando FALCÓN Y TELLA, Published in the *Anuario de Derechos Humanos, Nueva Época*, Instituto de Derechos Humanos, Facultad de Derecho, Universidad Complutense de Madrid, 5, 2004, pp. 369-386.

LEFÈBVRE, Henri, *Vers le cybernanthrope*, Paris, Denoël & Gonthier, 2000.

LIROLA DELGADO, Isabel – MARTÍN MARTÍNEZ Magdalena, *La Corte Penal Internacional: justicia versus impunidad*, Barcelona, Ariel, 2001.

LISÓN ARCAL, José C., *La globalización que nos quieren vender*, Madrid, Nivela, 2003.

LOCATELLI, Pia, "Globalización, un proceso en marcha", in Dolors RENAU (comp.), Micaela NAVARRO (et al.), *Globalización y mujer*, Madrid, Pablo Iglesias, 2002.

LÓPEZ, Alfonso – GÁLVEZ, Pepe, *La globalización: pasen y vean*, Barcelona, Icaria, 2002.

LÓPEZ CALERA, Nicolás (ed.), *La palabra contra el terrorismo*, Granada, 2004.

LÓPEZ CALERA, Nicolás, *¿Es posible un mundo justo? Estudios de Filosofía jurídica y política*, Granada, Universidad de Granada, 2003.

LÓPEZ GARRIDO, Diego, *Terrorismo, política y derecho: la legislación antiterrorista en España, Reino Unido, República Federal de Alemania, Italia y Francia*, Madrid, Alianza, 1987.

LÓPEZ PERONA, Alfonso, "Tres experiencias pluriculturales: India, EEUU, Perú", in BADILLO O'FARRELL, Pablo (comp.), *Pluralismo, tolerancia, multiculturalismo…, op. cit.*, pp.143-173.

LOSANO, Mario G., *Corso di Informatica giuridica, vol. I, Informatica per le scienze sociali*, Torino, Einaudi, 1985; *vol. II, 1, Il diritto privatto dell'informatica*, Torino Einaudi, 1986; *vol. II. 2, Il diritto pubblico dell'informatica*, Torino, Einaudi, 1986.

LUCAS, Javier de, *Globalización e identidades: claves políticas y jurídicas*, Barcelona, Icaria, 1rst ed., 2003.

LUCAS, Javier de (*et al.*), *La multiculturalidad*, Madrid, Consejo General del Poder Judicial, 1rst ed., 1rst reprint, 2002.

LUCAS MURILLO DE LA CUEVA, Pablo, *El derecho a la autodeterminación informativa*, Madrid, Tecnos, 1990.

LYNCH, J., "Crime in International Perspective", in James Q. WILSON – Joan PETERSILIA (eds.), *Crime*, San Francisco, CA, Institute of Contemporary Studies, 1995, pp. 11-39.

MacLENNAN, G., *Pluralism*, London, Open University Press, 1995.

MAESSO CORRAL, María – GONZÁLEZ BLANCO, Raquel (comps.), *La globalización, oportunidades y desafíos*, Cáceres, Universidad de Extremadura, Servicio de Publicaciones, 2003.

MALEM SEÑA, Jorge Francisco, *Globalización, comercio internacional y corrupción*, Barcelona, Gedisa, 2000.

MANN, Michael (*et al.*), *La globalización y el 11 de septiembre*, Madrid, Akal, 2001.

MARCUSE, Herbert, *One-Dimensional Man. Studies in the Ideology of Advanced Industrial Society*, London, Routledge & Kegan Paul, 1964.

MÀRIA I SERRANO, Josep F., *La globalización*, Barcelona, Christianisme i Justicia, D. L., 2000.

MARÍ SÁEZ, Víctor Manuel, *Globalización, nuevas tecnologías y comunicación*, Madrid, Ediciones de la Torre, 1999.

MARTÍN, Victoriano, "Globalización, reo o fiscal", in Paloma de VILLOTA (ed.), *Globalización a qué precio: el impacto en las mujeres del norte y del sur*, Barcelona, Icaria Antrazyt, 2001.

MARTÍN LÓPEZ, Enrique: *La sociedad global.* Madrid. Fundación para la Formación de Altos Profesionales. 1997.

MARTÍNEZ, Daniel – VEGA RUÍZ, María Luz, *La globalización gobernada: estado, sociedad y mercado en el siglo XXI*, Madrid, Tecnos, 2001.

MARTÍNEZ DE BRINGAS, Asier, *Globalización y derechos humanos*, Bilbao, Universidad de Deusto, 2001.

MARTÍNEZ MUÑOZ, Juan Antonio, "Guerra y Derecho internacional", in Various Authors, *Guerra, Moral y Derecho*, Madrid, Actas, 1994, pp. 85-109.

- *¿Abuso del Derecho?*, Madrid, Servicio de Publicaciones, Facultad de Derecho, Universidad Complutense de Madrid, 1999.

- "Multiculturalismo y estados personales", in *Anuario de Derechos Humanos, Nueva Época, Volumen 2*, Instituto de Derechos Humanos, Facultad de Derecho, Universidad Complutense de Madrid, Madrid, 2001, pp. 779-837.

MARTINS GARCÍA LEITE, Isabela, *Tribunal Penal Internacional como una contribución real a la paz y a la seguridad de la humanidad en el ámbito de la Organización de las Naciones Unidas*, Instituto de Derechos Humanos, Facultad de Derecho, Universidad Complutense de Madrid, Thesis directed by Manuel PÉREZ GONZÁLEZ, 1997. Unpublished.

MENDIZABAL, Antxon, *La globalización: perspectivas desde Euskal Herría*, Hondarribia, Hiru, 1999.

MENDUS, S. – EDWARDS, D., *On toleration*, Oxford, Oxford University Press, 1987.

MEZZADRA, Sandro, *Derecho de fuga. Migraciones, ciudadanía y globalización*, Spanish translation by Miguel SANTUCHO, Madrid, Traficantes de Sueños, 2005.

MICHELMANN, Hans J., (*et al.*), *Globalization and Agricultural Trade Policy*, Boulder Co., Lynne Rienner Publishers, 2001.

MIR PUIGPELAT, Oriol, *Globalización, Estado y Derecho. Las transformaciones recientes del Derecho administrativo*, Madrid, Civitas, 2004.

MITTELMAN, James H. (ed.), *Globalization*, Boulder, Lynne Rienner, 1997.

MOLINA IBAÑEZ, Mercedes, *La globalización económica a debate*, Madrid, Instituto Complutense de Estudios Internacionales, 1998.

MONTES MENDOZA, Rosa Isabel (comp.), *Globalización y nuevas tecnologías: nuevos retos y ¿nuevas reflexiones?*, Madrid, Organización de Estados Iberoamericanos para la Educación, la Ciencia y la Cultura, 2001.

MORALEDA, Inma, "Globalización y proximidad", in Dolors RENAU (comp.), *Globalización y mujer*, Madrid, Pablo Iglesias, 2002.

MORENO DOMÍNGUEZ, Juan Francisco, "La Carta de los Derechos Fundamentales de la Unión Europea: desde la solemnidad a la eficacia", in *Derecho y conocimiento*, vol. 2, pp. 325-347. Awarded with the Prize: *Sapere Aude*, 2003.

MULTICULTURALISMO Y DIFERENCIA. *Anales de la Cátedra Francisco Suárez*, 31, 1994.

MUÑOZ ALONSO, Alejandro, *El terrorismo en España*, Barcelona, Planeta, 1982.

MUSIL, Robert, *Der Mann ohne Eigenschaften*, Hamburg, Rowohlt, 1952.

NAVARRO, Vicenç (1937-), *Globalización económica, poder político y Estado del Bienestar*, Barcelona, Ariel, 2000.

NEBASKUES, Iker, *Globalización y nueva política local*, Bilbao, Instituto Vasco de Administración Pública, 2003.

NUÑEZ FLORENCIO, Rafael, *El terrorismo anarquista: (1888-1909)*, Madrid, Siglo Veintiuno, 1983.

NUSSBAUM, Martha, *Los límites del patriotismo. Identidad, pertenencia y "ciudadanía mundial"*, Spanish translation by C. CASTELLS, Barcelona, Paidós, 1999.

OBSTFELD, Maurice – TAYLOR, Alan M., *Globalization and Capital Markets*, Cambridge –Massachusetts-, National Bureau of Economic Research, 2002.

OLASOLO, Héctor, *Corte Penal Internacional ¿dónde investigar?: especial referencia a la Fiscalía en el proceso de activación*, preface by María del Carmen CALVO SÁNCHEZ, foreword by José Luis RODRÍGUEZ-VILLASANTE Y PRIETO, introduction by Juan Antonio YÁÑEZ-BARNUEVO, Valencia, Tirant Lo Blanch, 2003.

OLIET PALÁ, Alberto (coord.), *Globalización, Estado y democracia*, Málaga, Universidad de Málaga, Servicio de Publicaciones, 2003.

OLIVIÉ ALDASORO, Iliana, *Globalización financiera y crisis en economías emergentes: análisis teórico y estudio de los casos de México (1994) y Corea del Sur (1997)*, Thesis, Universidad Complutense de Madrid, Facultad de Ciencias Económicas y Empresariales, Departamento de Economía Aplicada I. Directed by Pablo BUSTELO GÓMEZ, 2002. Madrid, Servicio de Publicaciones de la Universidad Complutense de Madrid, 2004.

ORTEGA, Concepción – GUERRA, María José (comps.); AGRA, María Xosé (*et al.*), *Globalización y neoliberalismo: ¿un futuro inevitable?*, Oviedo, Nobel, 2002.

ORTEGA RIQUELME, Eugenio, *La globalización en la encrucijada: sociedad, política y mercado en un mundo globalizado*, Buenos Aires, Lom, 2002.

ORWELL, George, *1984*, Barcelona, Destino, 5rst ed., 1980.

O'SULLIVAN, Noel (*et al.*), *Terrorismo, ideología y revolución*, Spanish trans. by Néstor A. MÍGUEZ, Madrid, Alianza, 1987.

OST, François, "Mundialización, globalización y universalización: Abandonar, ahora y siempre, el estado de naturaleza", in *Anuario de Derechos Humanos, Nueva Época*, vol. 3, Instituto de Derechos Humanos, Facultad de Derecho, Universidad Complutense, Madrid, 2002, pp. 453-493.

PALAZUELOS MANSO, Enrique, *La globalización financiera: la internalización del capital financiero a finales del siglo XX*, Madrid, Síntesis, 1998.

PARAMIO, Ludolfo, "Globalización, movimientos sociales y partidos políticos", in Micaela NAVARRO (*et al.*), *Globalización y mujer*, Madrid, Pablo Iglesias, 2002.

PARDO, María Laura – NOBLIA, María Valentina (eds.); ARANOVICH, Laura (*et al.*), *Globalización y nuevas tecnologías*, Buenos Aires, Biblos, 2000.

PAREKH, B., *Rethinking Multiculturalism. Cultural Diversity and Political Theory*, London, 2000; there is Spanish translation, *Repensando el multiculturalismo. Diversidad cultural y teoría política*, Madrid, Istmo.

PELÁEZ MARÓN, José (comp.), *Globalización, deuda externa y exigencias de justicia social*, Tres Cantos (Madrid), Akal, 2003.

PEREYRA, Diego, *Globalización, hegemonía y crisis: una mirada crítica sobre la globalidad y las transformaciones del capitalismo mundial*, Buenos Aires, Eudeba, 1999.

PÉREZ HERNÁNDEZ, Pedro P. – ROMERO RODRÍGUEZ, José J. (dirs.), *Globalización de los mercados y crisis agraria: perspectivas para la agricultura andaluza*, Córdoba, Publicaciones Etea, 1996.

PÉREZ LUÑO, Antonio-Enrique, *Manual de Informática y Derecho*, Barcelona, Ariel, 1996.

- *¿Ciberciudadanía@ o ciudadanía@com?*, Barcelona, Gedisa, 2004.

- *La tercera generación de derechos humanos*, Navarra, Thomson-Aranzadi, 2006.

PIZZOLO, Calogero, *Globalización e integración: ensayo de una teoría general: Comunidad Andina, MERCOSUR, Unión Europea, Sica*; Buenos Aires, EDIAR, 2002.

PORRAS LEAL, Deysi Yolima, *La creación de la Corte Penal Internacional*, Instituto de Derechos Humanos, Facultad de Derecho, Universidad Complutense de Madrid, directed by Manuel PÉREZ GONZÁLEZ, 1999. Thesis unpublished.

PORTO ALEGRE, GLOBALIZAR LA ESPERANZA: TEXTOS DE NOAM CHOMSKY Y JOSÉ SARAMAGO, SÍNTESIS DE CONFERENCIAS Y DECLARACIONES DEL II FORO SOCIAL MUNDIAL REALIZADO EN PORTO ALEGRE, BRASIL, Santiago de Chile, Aún creemos en los sueños, 2002.

QUEL LÓPEZ, J. (ed.), *Creación de una jurisdicción penal internacional*, Madrid, AEPDIRI / BOE / Escuela Diplomática, 2000, Colección Escuela Diplomática, 4.

RAGUÉS I VALLÈS, Ramón, *El Tribunal Penal Internacional: la última gran institución del siglo XX*, Madrid, La Ley. Diario 2001.

RAI, Milan, *Plan de guerra contra Irak: diez razones para no iniciar una nueva guerra contra Irak;* with a chapter by Noam CHOMSKY, Spanish translation by Juan Mari MADARIAGA, edited by Carlos PRIETO DEL CAMPO, Madrid, Foca, 2003.

RAMÓN CHORNET, Consuelo, *Terrorismo y respuesta de fuerza en el marco del Derecho internacional,* Valencia, Tirant Lo Blanch, 1993.

RAMONET, Ignacio, "¡Nos han robado la esperanza!", in "Internet, ¿un bien o una maldición?", in *El País Digital-Debates,* 25 February 1997.

RAMOS TORRE, Ramón – GARCÍA SELGAS, Fernando (eds.), *Globalización, riesgo, reflexividad: tres temas de la teoría social contemporánea,* Madrid, Centro de Investigaciones Sociológicas, 1999.

RAZ, Joseph, *The Morality of Freedom,* Oxford, Oxford University Press, 1986.

- *Ethics in the Public Domain: Essays in the Morality of Law and Politics,* Oxford, Clarendon Press; New York, Oxford University Press, 1994.

RAWLS, John (1921-2002), *Political Liberalism,* New York, Columbia University Press, 2005.

REINARES, Fernando, *Terrorismo y antiterrorismo,* Barcelona, Paidós, 1998.

- *Terrorismo global,* Madrid, Taurus, 2003.

RENAU, Dolors (comp.); NAVARRO, Micaela (*et al.*), *Globalización y mujer,* Madrid, Pablo Iglesias, 2002.

RIBERO, Isel, "Globalización, desigualdad y mujer", in Micaela NAVARRO (*et al.*), Dolors RENAU (comp.), *Globalización y mujer,* Madrid, Pablo Iglesias, 2002.

ROBLES MORCHÓN, Gregorio, *Crimen y castigo (Ensayo sobre Durkheim),* Madrid, Civitas, 2001.

RUBIO-CARRACEDO, José, "Pluralismo, multiculturalismo y ciudadanía compleja", in BADILLO O'FARRELL, Pablo (coord.), *Pluralismo, tolerancia, multiculturalismo,* op. cit., pp. 173-195.

SALAZAR MENDIGUCHIA, Pablo, *Globalización con desarrollo local. Entrevista, Gustavo González,* Barcelona, Icaria, 2002.

SALINAS DE FRÍAS, Ana (comp.), *Nuevos retos del Derecho: integración y desigualdades desde una perspectiva comparada Estados Unidos-Unión Europea,* Málaga, Universidad de Málaga, 2001.

SÁNCHEZ INAREJOS, Juan José, *La globalización al desnudo: un viaje desde la realidad económica y tecnológica hasta lo más íntimo del corazón humano,* Madrid, Chaos-Entropy, D. L., 2001.

SÁNCHEZ PATRÓN, José Manuel, *Las organizaciones internacionales ante las violaciones de los derechos humanos,* Oviedo, Septem Ediciones, 2004.

SANGUINETTI RAYMOND, Wilfredo – GARCÍA LASO, Agustín (eds.), *Globalización económica y relaciones laborales,* Salamanca, Universidad de Salamanca, 2003.

SANTOS, Boabentura de Sousa, *La globalización del Derecho: los nuevos caminos de la regulación y la emancipación,* Spanish trans. by César RODRÍGUEZ, Bogotá, Facultad de Derecho, Ciencias Políticas y Sociales, Universidad Nacional de Colombia, 1998, 1rst ed., 2nd reprint., 2002.

SANTOS GRANERO, Fernando (comp.), *Globalización y cambio en la Amazonía indígena,* Quito, Abya-Yala, 1996.

SARTORI, Giovanni, *Homo videns. La sociedad teledirigida,* Madrid, Taurus, 1998.

- *La sociedad multiétnica. Pluralismo, multiculturalismo y extranjeros,* Madrid, Taurus, 2001.

SAXE-FERNÁNDEZ, John (comp.), *Globalización: crítica a un paradigma,* México, Universidad Nacional Autónoma de México, Plaza & Janés, 1999.

SAXE-FERNÁNDEZ, John – PETRAS, James – VELTMEYER, Henry - NUÑEZ, Omar, *Globalización, imperialismo y clase social,* Buenos Aires-México, Úmen, 2001

SCHACHAR, Ayelet, "Multicultural Vulnerability", in Christian JOPPKE – Steven LUKES (eds.), *Multicultural Questions, op. cit.,* pp. 87-111.

SCHOLTE, Jan Aart, *Globalization: a Critical Introduction*, London, MacMillan Press, 2000.

SEMINARIO DE ESTUDIOS INTERNACIONALES "LUIS DE MOLINA" (1. 2003. Cuenca), *Globalización y Derecho: reflexiones desde el Seminario...* Chairmen, Juan Ignacio CATALINA AYORA and Juan Miguel ORTEGA TEROL, Cuenca, Ediciones de la Universidad de Castilla-La Mancha, 2003.

SEMPRINI, Andrea, *Le multiculturalisme*, Paris, Presses Universitaires de France, 2000.

SEN, Amartya Kumar, "Democracia y desarrollo. Derechos del hombre y diferencias culturales", Spanish translation by José ITURMENDI MORALES, in *Anuario de Derechos Humanos, Nueva Época*, Instituto de Derechos Humanos, Universidad Complutense de Madrid, 1, 2000, pp. 367-387.

SENGENBERGER, Werner, *Globalización y progreso social: la función y el impacto de las normas internacionales del trabajo*, Caracas, Nueva Sociedad, Programa Sindical Regional, 2004.

SERRANO RUIZ-CALDERÓN, José Miguel, "La guerra y la justificación de la muerte del inocente en el Mundo contemporáneo", in Various Authors, *Guerra, Moral y Derecho*, Madrid, Actas, pp. 71-83.

- *Familia y Tecnología*, Madrid, Servicio de Publicaciones, Facultad de Derecho, Universidad Complutense de Madrid, 1996.

- *Eutanasia y vida dependiente. Inconvenientes jurídicos y consecuencias sociales de la despenalización de la eutanasia*, Madrid, Ediciones Internacionales Universitarias, 1rst ed., enero 2001.

SEVILLA, José M., "Algunas raíces filosóficas del pluralismo en la modernidad", in BADILLO O'FARRELL, Pablo (comp.), *Pluralismo, tolerancia, multiculturalismo...*, op. cit., pp. 195-233.

SORIANO, Ramón, *Interculturalismo. Entre Liberalismo y Comunitarismo*, Córdoba, Almuzara, 2004.

SOROS, George, *Globalización*, Spanish translation by Rafael SANTANDREU LORITE, Barcelona, Planeta, 2002.

STERN, Jessica, *El terrorismo definitivo: cuando lo impensable sucede*, Barcelona (...), Granica, 2001.

SUÁREZ COLLÍA, José María, *La retroactividad. Normas jurídicas retroactivas e irretroactivas*, Madrid, Editorial Universitaria Ramón Areces, 1rst ed., December 2005; 1rst reprint, April 2006.

SUNSTEIN, Cass, *Republic.com*, Princeton, Princeton University Press, 2001; Spanish translation by P. GARCÍA SEGURA, Barcelona, Paidós, 2003.

SUÑÉ LLINÁS, Emilio, "Introducción a la informática jurídica y al Derecho de la informática", in *Informática y Derecho, Revista de la Facultad de Derecho de la Universidad Complutense de Madrid*, 12, 1986, pp. 65-79.

- "Bases de datos normativas", in *Civitas. Revista Española de Derecho Administrativo*, 45, 1989, pp. 85-110.

- *Informática práctica para juristas y profesionales del mundo de las letras*, Madrid, Servicio de Publicaciones, Facultad de Derecho, Universidad Complutense de Madrid, 1994.

- *La sociedad civil en la cultura postcontemporánea*, Madrid, Servicio de Publicaciones, Facultad de Derecho, Universidad Complutense de Madrid, 1998.

TAIBO, Carlos, *Globalización neoliberal y hegemonía de Estados Unidos*, Madrid, Arco Libros, 2003.

TAPIA VALDÉS, Jorge A., *El terrorismo de Estado: la doctrina de la seguridad nacional en el cono sur*, Caracas, Nueva Sociedad; México, DF, Editorial Nueva Imagen, 1980.

TAYLOR, Charles, *Multiculturalism and the Politics of Recognition*, Princeton, NJ, Princeton University Press, 1992.

- "The Politics of Recognition", in A. GUTMANN (ed.), *Multiculturalism*, Princeton, NJ, 1994.

TERRADILLOS BASOCO, Juan, *Terrorismo y derecho: comentario a las leyes orgánicas 3 y 4-1988, de reforma del Código Penal y de la Ley de Enjuiciamiento Criminal*, Madrid, Tecnos, 1988.

TERRORISMO, Madrid, Ministerio de Defensa, Centro Superior de Información de la Defensa, 1979.

TERRORISMO Y MEDIOS DE COMUNICACIÓN SOCIAL, Madrid, Ministerio del Interior, Secretaría General Técnica, 1984.

TERTSCH, Hermann, "¿Hacia un nuevo orden mundial?", in BADILLO O'FARRELL, Pablo (comp.), *Pluralismo, tolerancia, multiculturalismo..., op. cit.*, pp.233-245.

TOMLINSON, John, *Globalización y cultura*, Spanish translation by Fernando MARTÍNEZ VALDÉS, revision by José Luis GONZÁLEZ MARTÍNEZ, México, Oxford University Press, 2001.

TORIBIO, Juan José, *Globalización, desarrollo y pobreza*, Madrid, Círculo de Empresarios, 2003.

TORRE MARTÍNEZ, José de la, "La guerra subversiva o revolucionaria", in Various Authors, *Guerra, Moral y Derecho*, Madrid, Actas, pp. 137-161.

TORRES SANTOMÉ, Jurjo, *Globalización e interdisciplinariedad: el currículo integrado*, Madrid, Ediciones Morata, 1994; 2nd ed. 1996.

TOYNBEE, Arnold Joseph (1889-1975), *El terrorismo alemán en Bélgica: narración basada en los documentos*, introduction by Ramiro de MAEZTU, London, Hayman, Christy & Lilly, 1917.

URIARTE, Edurne, *Terrorismo y democracia tras el 11-M*, Madrid, Espasa Calpe, 2004.

VALERO FERNÁNDEZ DE PALENCIA, Ana, "Crónica del Curso 'Criterios Biojurídicos ante la Revolución Tecnológica'", in *Anuario de Derechos Humanos, Nueva Época*, Facultad de Derecho, Universidad Complutense de Madrid, 3, 2002, pp. 561-590.

VARGAS-MACHUCA ORTEGA, Ramón, "Orden político y justicia frente al terrorismo global. A propósito del 11-S", in BADILLO O'FARRELL, Pablo (comp.), *Pluralismo, tolerancia, multiculturalismo..., op. cit.*, pp. 245-260.

VASAK, Karel, *Pour les droits de l'homme de la troisième génération*, Strasbourg, Institut International des Droits de l'Homme, 1979.

- "Pour une troisième génération des droits de l'homme", in *Etudes et essais sur le droit international humanitaire et sur les principes de la Croix-Rouge en l'honneur de Jean Pictet*, La Haye, Mouton, 1984.

VEGA GARCIA, Pedro de, «Globalización y Derecho Internacional», in *Revista de Estudios Políticos*, 100.

VILLOTA, Paloma de (ed.), *Globalización y género*, preface by José Luis SAMPEDRO, Madrid, Síntesis, 1999.

- *Globalización a qué precio: el impacto en las mujeres del norte y del sur*, Barcelona, Icaria Antrazyt, 2001.

VENANZI, Augusto de (1950-), *Globalización y corporación: el orden social en el siglo XXI*, Rubí (Barcelona), Anthropos; Caracas, Universidad Central de Venezuela, 2002.

VILLAGRASA, Jesús, *Globalización: ¿un mundo mejor?*, México, Trillas, 2003.

VARIOUS AUTHORS, *Guerra, Moral y Derecho*, Madrid, Actas, 1994.

- *Hacia una justicia internacional*, Madrid, Ministerio de Justicia, BSCH, Civitas, 2000.

- *La criminalización de la barbarie: la Corte Penal Internacional*, Madrid, Consejo General del Poder Judicial, 2000.

YOUNG, Iris Marion, *Justice and the Politics of Difference*, Princeton, NJ, Princeton University Press, 1990.

YÚDICE, George, *Globalización de la cultura y nueva sociedad*, Caracas, Cipost, 1997.

WALDRON, Jeremy, "Minority Cultures and the Cosmopolitan Alternative", in Will KYMLICKA (ed.), *The Rights of Minority Cultures*, *op. cit.*, pp. 93-119.

WALZER, Michael, *On Toleration*, New Haven, Yale University Press, 1997.

WARLAW, Grant, *Terrorismo político: teoría, táctica y contramedidas*, Madrid, Estado Mayor del Ejército, 1986.

WATERS, Malcolm (1946-), *Globalization*, London, Routledge, 1995. 2nd ed., 2001.

WIEVIORKA, Michel, *El terrorismo: la violencia política en el mundo*, Closing words to this edition by Mario ONAINDÍA and Jorge M. REVERTE, Spanish translation by Regina MARTÍNEZ, Esplugues de Llobregat, Plaza y Janés, 1991.

WILKINSON, Paul, *Terrorismo político*, Madrid, Felmar, 1976.

ZICCARDI CAPALDO, Giuliana, *Terrorismo internazionale e garanzie collective*, Milano, Giuffrè, 1990.

Index

Nijhoff Law Specials

60. S. Skaale (ed.): *The Right to National Self-Determination: The Faroe Islands and Greenland*. 2004 ISBN 90 04 14207 X
61. E. McWhinney: *The September 11 Terrorist Attacks and the Invasion of Iraq in Contemporary International Law: Opinions on the Emerging New World Order System*. 2004 ISBN 90 04 14143 X
62. B.G. Ramcharan, *The Protection Role of National Human Rights Institutions*. 2005. ISBN 90 04 14526 5
63. C. de Cooker, *Accountability, Investigation and Due Process in International Organizations*. 2005. ISBN 90 04 14793 4
64. P. S. Jones & K. Stokke, *Democratising Development: The Politics of Socio-Economic Rights in South Africa*. 2005. ISBN 90 04 14821 3
65. R. S. Lee (ed.): *Swords Into Plowshares: Building Peace Through the United Nations*. 2005. ISBN 90 04 15001 3
66. J.A. Bovenberg, *Property Rights in Blood, Genes & Data: Naturally Yours?* 2006 ISBN 90 04 15053 6
67. F. Hoffmeister: *Legal Aspects of the Cyprus Problem*. 2006 ISBN 978 9004152 23 6
68. R. Bredel: *The Ethical Economy of Conflict Prevention and Development*. 2006 ISBN 978 9004153 05 9
69. P. Nedergaard: *European Union Administration: Legitimacy and Efficiency*. 2007 ISBN 978 9004155 73 2
70. L.G. Loucaides: *The European Convention on Human Rights*. 2007 ISBN 978 90 04 15883 2
71. F. Falcón y Tella: *Challenges for Human Rights*. 2007 ISBN 978 9004 16022 4

For more titles in this series, consult our web site: **http://www.brill.nl**

MARTINUS NIJHOFF PUBLISHERS – LEIDEN • BOSTON

www.ingramcontent.com/pod-product-compliance
Lightning Source LLC
Chambersburg PA
CBHW031327230926
51848CB00001B/119
* 9 7 8 9 0 0 4 1 6 0 2 2 4 *